StyleCity
PARIS

StyleCity
PARIS
THIRD EDITION

With over 400 colour photographs and 7 maps

Thames & Hudson

Contents

Street Wise

Style Traveller

Series concept and editor: Lucas Dietrich
Research and texts: Phyllis Richardson
Restaurant consultant and texts: Sébastien Demorand
Jacket and book design: Grade Design Consultants
Original design: The Senate
Maps: Peter Bull

Specially commissioned photography by
Anne and Philippe Croquet-Zouridakis,
Ingrid Rasmussen, Anthony Webb and Angela Moore

The **StyleCity** series is a completely independent guide.

Every effort has been made to ensure that the
information in this book is as up-to-date and as
accurate as possible at the time of going to press,
but some details are liable to change.

First published in the United Kingdom in 2003 by
Thames & Hudson Ltd, 181A High Holborn,
London WC1V 7QX

thamesandhudson.com

British Library Cataloguing-in-Publication Data
A catalogue record for this book is available from the
British Library

ISBN 978-0-500-21023-9

Printed in China by C & C Offset Printing Co Ltd

How to Use This Guide

The book features two principal sections: **Street Wise** and **Style Traveller**.

Street Wise, which is arranged by neighbourhood, features areas that can be covered in a day (and night) on foot and includes a variety of locations – cafés, shops, restaurants, museums, performance spaces, bars – that capture local flavour or are lesser-known destinations.

The establishments in the **Style Traveller** section represent the city's best and most characteristic locations – 'worth a detour' – and feature hotels (**sleep**), restaurants (**eat**), cafés and bars (**drink**), boutiques and shops (**shop**) and getaways (**retreat**).

Each location is shown as a circled number on the relevant neighbourhood map, which is intended to provide a rough idea of location and proximity to major sights and landmarks rather than precise position. Locations in each neighbourhood are presented sequentially by map number. Each entry in the **Style Traveller** has two numbers: the top one refers to the page number of the neighbourhood map on which it appears; the second number is its location.

For example, the visitor might begin by selecting a hotel from the **Style Traveller** section. Upon arrival, **Street Wise** might lead him to the best joint for coffee before guiding him to a house-museum nearby. After lunch he might go to find a special jewelry store listed in the **shop** section. For a memorable dining experience, he might consult his neighbourhood section to find the nearest restaurant cross-referenced to **eat** in **Style Traveller**.

Street addresses are given in each entry, and complete information – including email and web addresses – is listed in the alphabetical **contact** section. Travel and contact details for the destinations in **retreat** are given at the end of **contact**.

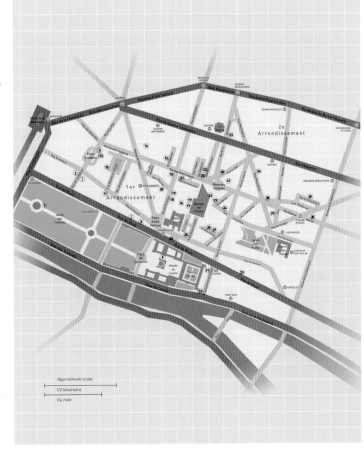

Legend

(**2**) Location

    Museums, sights

    Gardens, squares

(**M**) Métro stops

    Principal street

    Secondary road

PARIS

In the hearts and imaginations of people around the world, Paris, of all the great cities, hardly needs introduction. Even in those of us who have yet to set foot in the City of Lights, it is remembered as a beacon of artistic and literary endeavour after the war, a place where creativity and philosophy emanated from the cafés of the Left Bank like so much Gitanes cigarette smoke. 'Like Paris in the twenties', people say of any city drawing an international bohemian crowd with high culture on the cheap and high-intensity living to match. Yet no other city quite captures the particular 'romance' of Paris. This ineluctable appellation has perhaps become cliché, but the real thing is still there for the savvy visitor.

Like any ancient city, modern Paris is built on many layers and exists on many levels of perception: physical, historical, emotional. One reason that Paris retains its aura is, of course, its survival — more or less intact — through the great wars. Coveted by invaders who would rather own it than destroy it, it is a city marked by large personalities and grandiose expressions: from King Philippe-Auguste, who chartered the first university in the 13th century, and the spendthrift François I, who rebuilt the Louvre in Italian Renaissance style and promoted humanism, to the even more ostentatious Sun King, who left the Louvre in favour of Versailles, and Napoleon, who added his own imperial monuments: the Arc de Triomphe, the Arc du Carrousel, the column of the place Vendôme. It was his nephew, Napoleon III, who left probably the most visible urban legacy through the work of his urban engineer Georges (later Baron) Haussmann. Haussmann 'modernized' Paris, clearing away vast areas of medieval buildings (which historians decry to this day) to make way for the grand boulevards that give Paris so much of its opulent character, as well as building schools, churches and synagogues.

Modern democratic and coalition rulers were understandably more restrained than their autocratic predecessors, but the city has been touched by great architectural vision even in the late 20th century: Georges Pompidou's sponsorship of the ground-breaking 'high-tech' art centre (p. 80) designed by Richard Rogers and Renzo Piano in 1977, and Valéry Giscard d'Estaing's support for the audacious conversion of the Gare d'Orsay railway station into a celebration of art. In the 1980s and 1990s, Mitterand's controversial *grands projets* (the Bastille Opera House, the Grand Louvre project, the new library, the Grande Arche de la Défense) and the creation of large landscaped parks – André Citroën (p. 39) and Bercy (p. 100) – confirm a determination to ensure that Paris continues to embrace bold modernity and urban innovation. Though so much of the past has been preserved here, this is a cosmopolitan city at the forefront of fashion, design and the arts. Paris is where artists, musicians and writers flock to be inspired, to be with other creative minds. Is the love of beauty and style particularly French? Is the sense of romance engendered by past struggles, by strong traditions of language and culture? Almost as well known for the outspokenness of its citizenry as for its unparalleled sense of style, Paris's streets have been the scene of revolution, protests, foreign occupation, liberation and unbridled celebration, and they continue to be a public staging ground.

What visitors will find in Paris today is a city bursting with creative energy, not in the edgy, street-conscious way of, say, London, but in a manner reflecting a more artisanal – and at times flamboyant – attitude to creativity. The most talked-about hotels are lavishly decorated in the spirit of the Empire or in a particularly French brand of minimalism; the best restaurants combine the talents of the most innovative designers with young chefs trained in traditional French methods, but willing to experiment with global cuisines. The grand old fashion houses are still lined up around the Faubourg St-Honoré and the Champs-Élysées, but so are the new names, and in pockets around the Marais, the Bastille and Montmartre young designers with backroom ateliers are producing clothing, objects and furniture that you won't see anywhere else. The late-night club scene still thrives, reinvented, revitalizing the old cabarets of Montmartre and in the once-disused spaces around the Bastille and the République. Creative hopefuls have also flowed into and reinvigorated outer 'villages', such as Canal St-Martin and Belleville. Café culture throughout the capital is alive and well, with many a *terrasse* filled with conversation.

Paris, as writer Edmund White contends, is truly the city of the *flâneur*, where an aimless wander can bring unexpected rewards around every corner – the glimpse of a medieval square, an exquisite boutique, an enticing café, or one of those grand architectural gestures in which Paris's place in history and the imagination is writ large.

Street Wise

Latin Quarter
St-Germain-des-Prés
Montparnasse

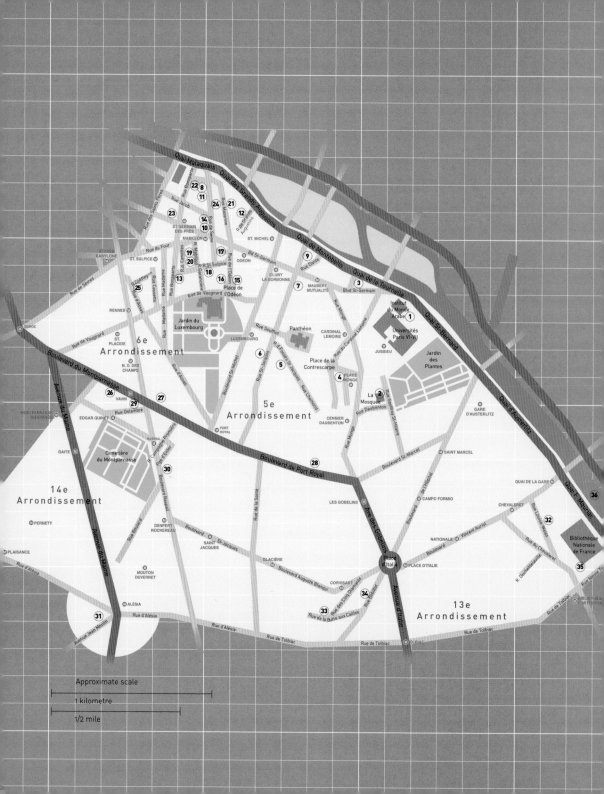

The Latin Quarter is where Paris's first university was founded in the 12th century. Latin was the language of learning, and so gave its name to an area focused on enlightenment. The neighbourhood today, bordered roughly by the contrasting but equally wonderful Jardin du Luxembourg and Jardin des Plantes, is still one of multicultural influences, of students and new bohemians. It is fitting that two of Paris's most significant Islamic institutions should be near this historic seat of learning. La Mosquée de Paris, built in the 1920s, was erected as a tribute to North African efforts in the First World War and its exquisite décor is the work of a multitude of the region's craftsmen. Its small tea salon (p. 150) brings a refreshing exoticism to the quarter. Farther north, on a picturesque quayside setting adjacent to the large modern university complex, the Institut du Monde Arabe (p. 17) shows the modern face of Islamic-French architecture with a technologically advanced design by Jean Nouvel. As a centre for art and culture, it exudes all the excitement of dedication and learning that has distinguished the quarter for centuries.

Another influential educational centre is several blocks west in St-Germain-des-Prés. The École des Beaux-Arts is a world-renowned institution that infuses the entire area with artistic aspirations, which, in turn, radiate throughout Paris and beyond. Now that its post-war literary associations have been overtaken by its modern design and art connections, the quarter is known for furnishings, decorative objects and art from the early to mid-20th century. In addition to being a home to the galleries, St-Germain-des-Prés has a reputation for its fine shopping district, filled with smart, artistically inclined boutiques, not the emerging talents found in Montmartre or even in parts of the Marais, but designers who have managed to achieve enough high-profile success to maintain a shop in this glittering neighbourhood.

Before you wander from the delights of St-Germain-des-Prés to the even more upmarket offerings of the Rue du Bac, dip south into the villagey streets of the Butte-aux-Cailles, especially around Montparnasse, long known as a bohemian enclave, and the rue des Cinq-Diamants (p. 26). Here are the less glamorous but equally important parts, picturesque old neighbourhoods with restaurants, cafés and streets that gain in character what they lose in urban frenzy. Over in the 13th, the area around the Bibliothèque Nationale is experiencing a burst of urban renewal celebrated by the Passarelle Simone de Beauvoir (p. 26), linking the newly popular riverside decks to the Parc de Bercy (p. 100) on the Right Bank.

1 Institut du Monde Arabe

1, rue des Fossés-St-Bernard, 5th

The centre for Arabic arts and culture was designed by French architect Jean Nouvel in 1987 around the concept of a *moucharabieh*, but with a distinctly modern twist: photo-electric cells in the exterior cladding adjust the amount of light entering the building to protect the museum pieces inside. There have been problems with some of the more technical aspects of the design – the cells don't always function perfectly – but the building itself is still a graceful piece of architecture, with Islamic elements and patterns woven into the modern white façade and the added appeal of the white-paved square spreading out to the road. Apart from the permanent collection of art, artefacts and decorative objects, the institute also hosts exhibitions and films, along with lectures on art, architecture, literature and history. The stylishly modern café Loubnane serves sandwiches and drinks.

HAMMAM AND MINT TEA
2 La Mosquée de Paris

FRESH BEGINNINGS
3 Le Petit Pontoise

9, rue de Pontoise, 5th

The last time we walked into this lovely bistro, we encountered a dozen baskets filled with fresh wild mushrooms (boletus, chanterelle); others contained sublimely red raspberries and dark blackberries. On another table were arranged *potimarrons* (small pumpkins with a chestnut flavour), Espelette pepper braids from the Pays Basque and two kilos of fresh walnuts. On a wall, a small sign reads: 'We'll start cooking once you've ordered. Please be patient.' If only such freshness of ingredients and scrupulousness could spread to every single bistro in the city. Try the plain and simple roasted chicken with purée; you'll never want to eat it anywhere else.

TEA CEREMONIES
4 La Maison des Trois Thés

TOUT LE JOUR
5 Café de la Nouvelle Mairie

19–21, rue des Fossés-St-Jacques, 5th

This colourful café is the kind of place you can visit at any time of day: for a cup of coffee with the newspapers around 9 am, for a quick bite at lunchtime, a beer at 4 in the afternoon, an apéritif with friends around 7. It is quite frankly a dream of a bistro, with a terrace facing a lovely little square, and people happily chatting on the bright green benches inside while being serenaded by jazzy background music. All of this is enhanced by a short but clever wine list (try a Morgon from the Beaujolais region or a Côteaux du Languedoc) and an irreproachable cuisine, essentially based on charcuterie or farm cheese plates and a *plat du jour*.

TASTEBUDS IN ECSTASY
6 Les Papilles

30, rue Gay-Lussac, 5th

Bertrand Bluy, former pastry chef at Le Bristol and Taillevent, left the world of Michelin two- and three-star enterprises to open this wonderful little gourmet shop and restaurant based on fantastic home-style cooking and a warm and inviting atmosphere. The shop area is filled with luxury foods sourced from around the country – soups, peppers, salt, jam – and is overflowing with well-chosen wines. The restaurant serves up a menu of modern, neo-bistro food, all much tastier than any of us could actually do at home. Dishes like Basque goat's cheese with black-cherry jam and Espelette pepper jelly, duck breast with butter-encrusted new potatoes, oysters and charcuterie are prepared and presented in copper cooking pots, contributing to the familiar feeling. In a neighbourhood somewhat lacking in inspired offerings, this is the choice of foodies in the know.

7   Le Pré Verre
8, rue Thénard, 5th

This is the kind of place where you can't even think about dropping in without notice. Whether for lunch or dinner, Le Pré Verre is simply always full. But it is well worth the effort of booking a table in advance to give yourself the chance to discover one of the best of the new Parisian bistros, set up by two brothers who are both passionate about cooking, spices and wine. You might try the cod served with smoked potato mash, or the suckling pig with crunchy cabbage and preserved lemon soup. Their dishes are in great demand, but they all come with a smile and adhere to the same overly modest claim of being cheap 'n' tasty. They are that, and a lot more.

MODERN FRENCH AND NEW-DESIGN FURNITURE
8   Alexandre Biaggi
14, rue de Seine, 6th

Alexandre Biaggi has been dealing in antique furniture since he hired a stand at the Marché aux Puces in 1987. Since 1989 he has had his own shop selling French 19th- and 20th-century furniture and objects, which he has refined even further to French design from the 1930s, 1940s and 1950s – Jean-Michel Frank, André Arbus and Jacques Adnet, as well as Paul Dupré-Lafon, Serge Roch, Jean Royère and Jacques Quinet, to name a few. In addition, he is the exclusive dealer in the work of contemporary designers Hervé van der Straeten and Nicolas Aubagnac.

OFFALLY GOOD
9   Ribouldingue
10, rue St-Julien-le-Pauvre, 5th

In the shade of Notre-Dame, the two ladies who run this pretty bistro (one in the dining room, the other at the stove) have decided to restore the dignity of offal cuisine — an old French tradition that has been mistreated by fashion, breaking the hearts of all aficionados of cow's udder salad, breaded pig's snout with mustard sauce and lamb's tongue in tartar sauce. Those who have no particular craving for organ meats can relax; you may also order generous non-offal dishes like root celery in *rémoulade* and jellied vegetables, or fresh cod with vegetables and pesto. For such a price, you may say this place is one of the best bargains in Paris.

GREAT GOURMAND
10   Da Rosa
62, rue de Seine, 6th

Even if your hotel has everything you could ever want, you should still stop by this deli of delights to pick up a snack or a great bottle of wine to sip beside the Seine. Gourmet grocer José da Rosa has spent years travelling the world to find produce for some of Paris's top kitchens, and now he has opened his larder and cellars to the public at large. The assortment and packaging of cheese, smoked meats and fish, olives, truffles and wine all displayed in the boutique and tasting room designed by Parisian star Jacques Garcia have refinement written all over them, so you'll be popular with gifts from these well-stocked shelves. You can also sit down and treat yourself to a plate from the menu.

BEAUX-ARTS BEAUTY
11   Galerie Doria
16, rue de Seine, 6th

This large gallery on the art-filled rue de Seine specializes in early 20th-century decorative arts, particularly works by members of the Union des Artistes Modernes. It is populated by a wealth of familiar names from the iconic period in French design: Pierre Chareau, Robert Mallet-Stevens, Le Corbusier, Charlotte Perriand, Eileen Gray. Furnishings, objects and sculpture with an architectural edge are laid out in an elegant, minimal space.

RAW ARTISTRY
12   Ze Kitchen Galerie
144

SWEET ARTS
13   Pierre Hermé
164

14 TO DRINK LIKE A …
14 Fish/La Boissonnerie
69, rue de Seine, 6th

If you've already been to Paris with a hip travel guide in your pocket, you might have run into this wine bar owned by a young American named Juan Sanchez (ask for the address of his wine shop), who knows French vineyards better than most French. Each week he changes the ten wines served by the glass, a clever means to ensure oenophiles return. His viticultural *coups de cœur* often take him to the Rhône valley, the Languedoc-Roussillon or the Riviera (check the fantastic Côtes de Provence Château de Roquefort, for instance). And to fill stomachs, the food is just right, mainly based on pasta and vegetables.

BUILDINGS BY THE BOOK
15 Librairie le Moniteur
7, place de l'Odéon, 6th

In its spacious modern premises on the place de l'Odéon, Librairie le Moniteur offers books on architecture, design and building, as well as sponsoring a number of its own publications – books, pamphlets, CD-ROMS – having started with the magazine *Moniteur des travaux publics* in 1903. Today this Parisian corner bookshop is an invaluable source for architecture, design and building enthusiasts.

SCULPTURE IN METALS AND GEMS
16 Galerie Hélène Porée
1, rue de l'Odéon, 6th

As you might expect from a jewelry shop that is called a gallery, there are pieces here that you could frame and hang on the wall, including architectural pieces, ones in trompe l'oeil that are cleverly faceted to appear more three-dimensional than they are, and those that are like jewel-topped sculpture. What you might not expect is that there are items that are very reasonably priced. The clear, elegant space is lined with cabinets of necklaces, earrings and rings by Alexandra Bahlmann, Cathy Chotard, Anuschka Wald, and Escher-like examples by Claude and Françoise Chavent. An upstairs room hosts exhibitions.

WINE AND WONDERMENT
17 Caves Miard

153

SOPHISTICATED FOLK
18 Vanessa Bruno
25, rue St-Sulpice, 6th

Vanessa Bruno's clothes have something of a 1970s gypsy look about them, but with a definite contemporary style. Blouses with lacy bodices, high necks and gathered sleeves are paired with bias-cut cardigans and flounced skirts. There is a range of chunky leather boots and bags, as well as more streamlined footwear, all with a relaxed attitude that's more folk than fashion. A pale yellow needlecord trouser suit with a black floral print is hard to resist, as are simple cotton T-shirts in subtle colours with lightly gathered necklines. This, Bruno's first shop, has homey, rough wood floors, but also a cut-out purple wall and funky ornamental chandelier to signal an all-over sense of design. Her newer shop on the pricey rue Castiglione goes more chic and modern with glossy white-enamel fixtures contrasting with the fresco-style wall treatments. Vanessa Paradis and Gwyneth Paltrow are reportedly fans of the Bruno mix of materials and styles.

JUST PLAIN GOOD
19 Les Charpentiers
10, rue Mabillon, 6th

One sometimes wonders why the city doesn't have more places like Les Charpentiers ('the carpenters'): a pleasant, old-fashioned décor, friendly waiters, affordable wines, customers from around the corner or from around the globe, and simple classic French food, quite well done: try some charcuteries, a tomato salad (with great olive oil, parsley and young white onions) or a blanquette 'Marie Louise', with its pieces of veal swimming in a generous creamy sauce, garnished with dots of carrots and button onions. Paris should always taste like this.

VINTAGE CHANEL
20 Les Trois Marches de Catherine B
1, rue Guisarde, 6th

If you have the bug for vintage designer wear, there are two necessary stops on your itinerary: Didier Ludot (p. 52) and Les Trois Marches. The two diminutive shopfronts on a narrow street near St-Sulpice conceal a wealth of clothing, handbags and accessories by Chanel, Louis Vuitton, and others presented and curated by Catherine B, who has amassed collections of such couture items as a splendid array of Hermès square scarves. She buys in items personally for the shop and also offers a few new pieces.

ARCHITECT-DESIGNED FURNITURE
21 Galerie 54
54, rue Mazarine, 6th

This is an area filled with galleries of every type but all are generally of a high quality, so collections need to be distinctive. Though this isn't the only gallery dealing in modern French design, it is one that does its job well. Eric Touchaleaume and Jean-Pierre Bouchard, its owners, specialize in 'furniture made by architects and in elements of architecture'. Charlotte Perriand, Jean Prouvé, Le Corbusier and Pierre Jeanneret are the focus of their collection, along with Serge Mouille, Georges Jouve and Alexandre Noll.

THE QUINTESSENCE OF ROMANCE
22 L'Hôtel
128

LITERARY STYLE
23 La Hune
170, boulevard St-Germain, 6th

A famed bookstore with notoriously late opening hours, La Hune is a white hub of culture on the *grand boulevard*. La Hune is known for its wide glass windows and white interior with discreet designerly elements, as well as for its art and design books. Books on art, style, architecture and graphics are carefully arranged on the galleried mezzanine level overlooking the street, while a good range of fiction (in French) is on the ground floor. A number of the titles upstairs are in English and quite a few are laid out on the counters under the windows, where you can browse and throw the occasional glance at the street scene below. Those suffering from vertigo might be wary of the slightly disconcerting angle of the stairs.

As the name suggests, La Palette is a café with genuine artistic leanings. Its proximity to the École des Beaux-Arts and setting in an area filled with galleries mean that it draws clientele from both. Large, colourful oil paintings and exhibition posters contribute to the arty Parisian stereotype. This is a traditional French café with all the classic offerings, occasionally brusque waiters and a fine corner spot for outdoor tables. The daily specials are fresh, well prepared and worth trying, even if you don't completely understand the description.

Some believe this is where you'll find Paris's best *sole meunière*. This 1930s brasserie is truly a top choice for upper-class fish and shellfish dishes. And there's the place itself: a breathtakingly beautiful Art Déco interior with velvet benches, black-and-white photos on the walls, plaques commemorating famous patrons (do you want to sit where Picasso sat, or perhaps Apollinaire?), and tuxedoed waiters moving silently from table to table. What to eat? Try *mouclade* (mussels in a fantastic creamy curry sauce), fried baby squid, sole (the fish is presented whole so the waiter can fillet it in front of you) or any kind of shellfish platter. Expensive, unforgettable.

27 Le Caméléon
6, rue de Chevreuse, 6th

True, the owner overacts a trifle, but let's face it – he knows his business. Jean-Paul Arabian hovers from table to table, says hello to the powerful and the anonymous on an equal basis, and has an irresistible way of presenting the day's menu: 'So, what did my chef prepare for you today? We have fried squid with a nice béarnaise sauce. Or some Basque pork, yes sir! With a side of carrots and pearl onions with coriander! Dessert, perhaps? Brioche French toast in a white beer *sabayon* sauce!' To make matters worse (or better), he's right most of the time and his pretty little bistro is always full. But do come for lunch, dinner being distinctly pricier.

PASTRY ARTS
28 Sadaharu Aoki
56, boulevard de Port Royal, 5th

Where else but in Paris would you find the Japanese skill of fine detailing turned to the art of pastry-making? Chef Sadaharu Aoki delights in what he calls France's 'treasure house of fruits', which he incorporates into many of his artful little delicacies, all set out in a suitably trim and elegant boutique that you would easily miss if you weren't looking out for it. Minute sketches that are works of art in themselves diagram the contents of some of the carefully stacked layers and swirls. Sesame and green tea are among the exotic flavours arranged in picture-perfect parcels. but he also turns out a number of more traditional items such as cheesecakes, millefeuille and a 'Japon', featuring strawberries and Chantilly cream. Aoki's confections are served in some of top Parisian tea houses, but there is also an elegant, if diminutive seating area here.

JAZZY CAFÉ
29 Rosebud
11 bis, rue Delambre, 14th

Here at this 1950s-style jazzy venue that attracts a crowd of thirty- to fifty-somethings, who come to drink cocktails and relive a certain dusky retro glamour, is reputedly where to find the best Bloody Mary in Paris, served by barmen in formal white jackets. The ambience has an American vibe, though there are plenty of locals to keep the dress-style elevated. Come in after a visit to the Fondation Cartier (see right) or cap your dinner at Le Dôme Montparnasse (p. 23) with an atmospheric post-prandial drink.

PATRONS OF CONTEMPORARY ART
30 Fondation Cartier
261, boulevard Raspail, 14th

With the Fondation Cartier pour l'art contemporain, architect Jean Nouvel has once again created a stand-out structure for a cultural centre. In 1994 the programme of corporate-sponsored arts moved into Nouvel's space of shifting glass panes, providing glimpses of the vibrant art scene inside. With the stated aim of 'building up a collection of work by living artists that is a reflection of the age', the foundation buys, commissions and exhibits, as well as staging theatre, music and dance performances. Artworks date from the 1980s, with French artists such as Arman César, Raymond Hains and Jean-Pierre Raynaud representing the commitment to national creativity, while an array of such international figures as Sam Francis, Joan Mitchell and James Turrell demonstrate Cartier's global mission 'to place modern art at the heart of the preoccupations of the modern world'.

SEASONAL PLEASURES
31 La Régalade

CUTTING-EDGE ART GALLERIES
32 Rue Louise-Weiss
- Galerie Praz-Delavallade, no. 28, 13th
- Galerie Kreo, no. 11, 13th
- Suzanne Tarasiève, 171, rue du Chevaleret, 13th

Together with rue Duchefdelaville and rue du Chevaleret, this seemingly unprepossessing street behind the Bibliothèque Nationale has become part of a new artistic quarter in Paris, showing its best face in monthly art fairs in which the galleries take part in joint public exhibitions. The galleries range from the modern-baroque Galerie Praz-Delavallade to the ultra-minimalist Galerie Kreo, featuring designs by hot Parisian duo Ronan and Erwan Bouroullec (see A-poc; p. 173). In the rue de Chevaleret, Suzanne Tarasiève represents an international roster of painters and sculptors, and has become a well-established stop on the European exhibition circuit. These are not the kinds of galleries you'll find around the Beaux-Arts: they are small, open infrequently, and show new blood. Taken in conjunction with a visit to the new happenings around the Bibliothèque Nationale, or to the Parc de Bercy (p. 100), or even on its own, it is a worthwhile pilgrimage for those looking to discover the current Parisian art scene. Exhibitions are not on a regular schedule; to find out more, check with the Louise 13 association ahead of time.

33 Rue de la Butte-aux-Cailles + Rue des Cinq-Diamants
Off rue Bobillot

- Chez Paul, 22, rue de la Butte-aux-Cailles, 13th
- Les Cailloux, 58, rue des Cinq-Diamants, 13th
- Suave, 20, rue de la Providence, 13th

Just south of the place d'Italie a confluence of pedestrianized streets shows a different side of Paris: a charming village full of lovely squares, small cafés and ethnic restaurants, students and local residents young and old. The atmosphere is much more casual and relaxed than the smarter and more touristy areas, and yet there is something to discover in a pleasant, quiet and characterful setting. Le Petite Alsace is a private street, but you can still have a polite look at the group of regional-style country houses. You might try dinner at Chez Paul, an old-fashioned restaurant with the feel of an old photograph, although it's a bit more modern than it looks. It's worth a try for age-old earthy classics like marrow bones, oxtail terrine, a great *pot au feu* (cheap but perfect beef cuts in a dense bouillon), milk-fed piglet roasted with sage, and the always delicious rum baba. Accompany these with a bottle of Mâcon or Chablis, and seize the day (or night). Those seeking a modern, Italian-influenced cuisine with an intelligent wine list popular with Parisians should head to Les Cailloux, where the two *rues* meet. Suave is a little eatery where the kitchen dishes up ultra-fresh Vietnamese and Thai cooking, as well as very exotic green jellied puddings.

34 L'Avant-Goût
26, rue Bobillot, 13th

For great contemporary French cooking at reasonable prices (though the price of the *prix fixe* menu nudges gently upwards, it remains one of the city's best bargains), it's worth seeking out this tiny, warm bistro near the Butte -aux-Cailles. There's no point in showing up without a booking, unless you're willing to start queuing outside two hours ahead of time for lunch or even longer for dinner. The place is always crowded, for everybody knows that chef Christophe Beaufront's market-bistro cuisine is both artful (the spicy *pot au feu* is the classic) and tasty, and that the welcome is always excellent.

35 MK2 Bibliothèque
128–162, avenue de France, 13th

In an out-of-the-way quayside location where the draw is mostly for the Bibliothèque Nationale or art lovers seeking out innovation around the rue Louise-Weiss (see p. 25), entertainment entrepreneur Marin Karmitz created the MK2 cinema complex, a place where the plastic, visual and design arts meet. Having over the last twenty-five years become the largest distributor of art-house features in France, Karmitz poured the resources of an empire into this building designed by Jean-Michel Wilmotte, with interiors, lighting, furniture and garden created specifically for this project by a host of known talents. The large, white 'futuristic-industrial' building includes fourteen screens, as well as four restaurants and up-to-date music and bookshops. The high-design theatres are angled to reduce any annoying head-blocking, and include specially commissioned, commodious red 'armchairs for two' by Martin Szekely. Added to the riverside library site, this mini city of art and design is helping to create a new artistic quarter in the 13th.

36 Passerelle Simone de Beauvoir
between quai de Bercy and quai François Mauriac, 13th

When François Mitterrand had the new Bibliothèque Nationale constructed as part of his scheme of *grands projets* throughout the capital, many criticized the design and the location, far from transportation and amenities. Ten years on, however, the hoped-for regeneration of the lower 13th is well under way. Architect-designed apartment blocks are springing up all around the new Métro stop and the old train station in this 'new part of Paris', as well as new university buildings and a floating swimming pool on the Seine. Some of the draw to the area is also due to the attractions offered by the MK2 cinema complex (see above), and though better quality eating and drinking venues haven't yet hit the neighbourhood, there is plenty of quayside atmosphere on the deck around the main library, which is now connected to the Right Bank at the quai de Bercy near the park (see p. 100). Designed by Austrian architect Dietmar Feichtinger for pedestrians and cyclists, the new bridge's gently undulating form can be entered at two levels and is meant to be used a public space as much as a utilitarian piece of infrastructure, so that those Parisian riverside essentials – the *bouquinistes* – can be accommodated as well as other stalls and exhibitions.

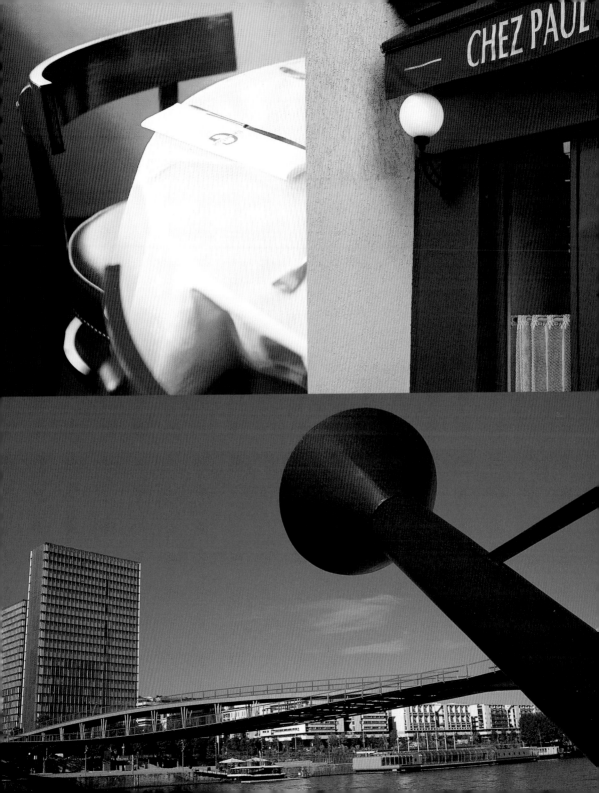

Rue du Bac
Chaillot
Champs-Élysées

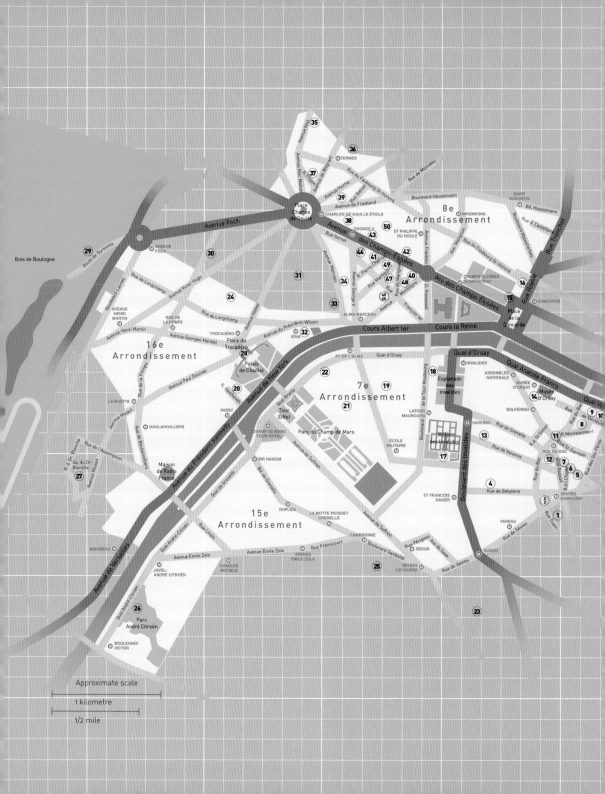

While the Right Bank can lay claim to an historic, royal air and some of the most classic and costly spots in Paris, the 7th Arrondissement has its own aristocratic attitude and luxe living, shopping and dining. An area of fine townhouses with even finer courtyard gardens, including a number of diplomatic residences, the Prime Minister's residence in the Hôtel Matignon (57, rue de Varenne), as well as government ministries, its main tourist spots are around the awe-inspiring Musée d'Orsay, Les Invalides and, of course, the Eiffel Tower. But the measure of the local population can be taken in the high-end design and fashion shops that cluster around the rue du Bac, leading off from the inimitable bourgeois emporium, Le Bon Marché (p. 163), Paris's first department store. You'll also find top-class independent French boutiques selling everything from haute couture to signature perfume to furnishings in retail spaces that comprise a *Who's Who* of French interior and architectural design: Philippe Starck, Christian Liaigre, Andrée Putman, Olivier de Lempeurer, Christian Biecher. While most of the grand old houses are private, one way to get an idea of what's behind the high walls is to visit restored house-museums like the 18th-century Hôtel Biron, now the Musée Rodin, and the Hôtel Bouchardon, now the Musée Maillol (p. 35). There is also a highly visible antiques route (see Carré Rive Gauche; p. 35) that now numbers over one hundred shops in the neighbourhood.

With the Eiffel Tower beckoning towards the Seine and the congestion of streets dispersing towards the southwest, a journey to the Parc André Citroën (p. 39) brings visitors from the small-scale perfection of the 7th to an open landscape that holds its own collection of wonders in an array of enchanting gardens: grand and airy, sculptural and poetic. If the weather is good, the detour is worth making, not least because it brings you near the gardens of another era, the Bois de Boulogne, a work of romantic 19th-century landscaping but also home to one of Paris's finest restaurants (see Le Pré Catalan; p. 141). The gastronomic tour continues, with culinary stars in the well-heeled southern 16th and around the Palais de Chaillot, which now houses the world's largest museum of architecture, while the city's largest contemporary art venue is enshrined in the nearby Palais de Tokyo (p. 39).

If you're feeling deprived of chic shopping here, you need only cross over on to the field of dreams that is the Champs-Élysées. Though it is constantly condemned for its unabashed over-commercialized character, it still draws people in droves. Get off the boulevard itself, and you'll discover interesting cafés, knockout bars and exquisite restaurants.

Dupin
aussi
tree
un plat

'BISTRONOMIC' BUSTLE

1 L'Épi Dupin

11, rue Dupin, 6th

Chef François Pasteau owns one of the city's typically 'bistronomic' venues, a place where one can find refined cuisine in a laid-back atmosphere. Hence the huge success of this pocket-sized restaurant near the Bon Marché (p. 163); don't even think about coming without booking your table at least a week before – especially if you want one of the tiny terrace tables in summer. Pasteau's culinary signature is a mix of French and international influences (he's worked in the US). Creative and pleasing, although the bustle isn't necessarily for everyone.

PARIS'S OLDEST DEPARTMENT STORE

2 Le Bon Marché

163

FASHION AND FOOD

3 Delicabar

Le Bon Marché, 1st floor, 7th

If anyone needed another reason to visit the Bon Marché (p. 163), here is one: a chic, in-store café designed by Claudio Colucci. Contoured furnishings, a round white bar dotted with red-seated stools (described as 'cherries on a cake'), and a courtyard terrace make for a cheerful and relaxed place in which to enjoy dishes by chef Sébastien Gaudard, former assistant to Pierre Hermé (p. 164). Offerings are in three varieties (fruits, legumes and chocolate), and in two options (sweet or savoury). Menu items printed in black, such as the chocolate foie gras, are savoury, while those in brown, like the decadent chocolate bubble, are, of course, sweet.

ORIENTALISM PAR EXCELLENCE

4 La Pagode

57 bis, rue de Babylone, 7th

An architectural curiosity built in 1896 by the wife of the entrepreneur behind the Bon Marché (p. 163), La Pagode began life as a Japanese-style *petite folie* before becoming a rather exotic movie theatre in 1931. Jean Cocteau premiered *Le Testament d'Orphée* here in 1959, and the venue was saved from demolition by director Louis Malle in the 1970s. Having been substantially renovated, today the venue features mainly alternative international films.

NEW COUTURE LINGERIE

5 Carine Gilson

174

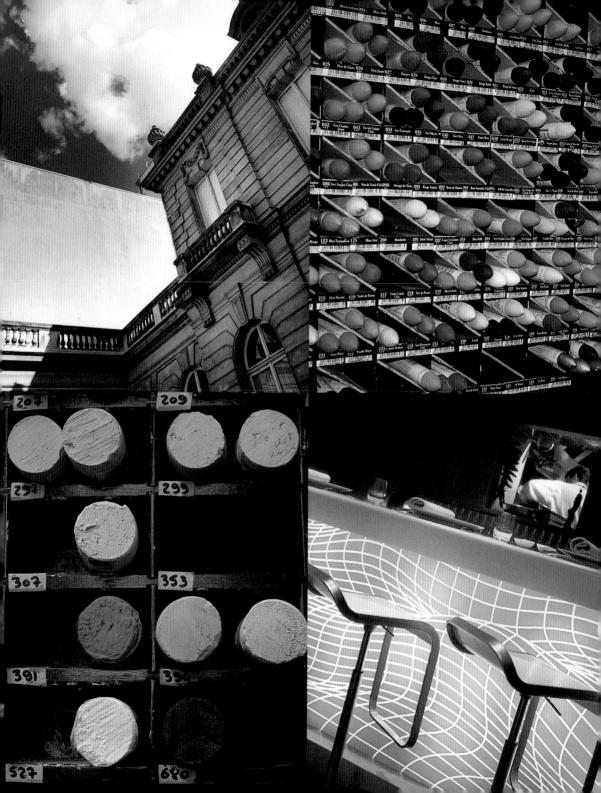

FASHION FIND
6 Ken Okada
1 bis, rue de la Chaise, 7th

The Paris-based Japanese designer first set up shop along with fellow *créateur* Sylviane Nuffer in the edgy design enclave of the rue des Gardes (p. 73), but she's come down the mountain and up into the big time with this shop near the rue de Grenelle. Expect lots of sharply cut black and white garments in contrasting fabrics and textures, with wraps and voluminous coats cut on the bias and using a luxurious amount of fabric. Dresses can be drapey and feminine, while the high collars and flared skirts of the coats and chemises are like a cross between high Victorian and Samurai warrior, never boring and like nothing else.

A WORLD-CLASS NOSE
7 Editions de Parfums Frédéric Malle

COOLEST CASHMERE
8 Lucien Pellat-Finet

ANTIQUES OF THE LEFT BANK
9 Carré Rive Gauche
between quai Voltaire and rue de l'Université, 7th

In an almost perfect square bordered by the quai Voltaire, rue des Sts-Pères, rue de l'Université and rue du Bac is a collection of streets in which antiques dealers banded together in the 1970s to promote their trade and to cooperate in group exhibitions, or 'open days', which now take place mainly in May. Today there are more than 100 dealers clustered into the area, and the events make for a lively influx of collectors from abroad. The organization remains active all year, and any shop sporting a Carré Rive Gauche emblem signals its participation and experience in the serious business of collecting.

MASTER COLOURER
10 Sennelier
3, quai Voltaire, 7th

Gustave Sennelier opened his first paint shop in 1887, and sold his own hand-ground pigments to top artists in the city. He later invented the metal tubes to replace pigs' bladders as handier and more robust containers, which were better at keeping the paints from hardening, an invention that helped boost the work of the Impressionists and other artists who painted in outdoor locations.

Sennelier's unique palette of inorganic colours was prized by artists such as Picasso, Bonnard and Cézanne, ensuring that some of the world's greatest museums are adorned with pigments by Sennelier. Today, the shop is still family run, with the affable Sophie Sennelier overseeing this historic and atmospheric emporium.

FANCIER FISH
11 Gaya Rive Gauche
44, rue du Bac, 7th

A themed makeover has created a glamorous underwater grotto with scales on the walls, seaweed-motif tables, bubble-patterned flooring and a bar base that seems to undulate beneath the counter. The interior was the work of Christian Ghion for Pierre Gagnaire, an international star who has taken his culinary talents far beyond his home country. The fare here is less pricey than at his eponymous eatery on the rue Balzac (p. 142), but it is still an upmarket experience. If you aren't prepared for the full-wave adventure, take a dip at the bar for oysters or a drink.

ARTISTIC LABOUR OF LOVE
12 Fondation Dina Vierny – Musée Maillol
59–61, rue de Grenelle, 7th

Aristide Maillol (1861–1944) met Dina Vierny when she was fifteen, and she became his model and close friend until his death ten years later. Vierny, who had also posed for Matisse and Bonnard, planned for thirty years to create a museum dedicated to an artist whose talent was not fully recognized during his lifetime. Opened in 1995, the museum contains the whole of Maillol's oeuvre, from drawings, engravings and paintings to his distinctive voluptuous sculptures, as well as pieces by contemporaries such as Rodin, Gauguin, Picasso, Degas and Cézanne. The museum also hosts temporary exhibitions.

VEGETABLE ARTS
13 L'Arpège
144

LAVISH LACROIX
14 Le Bellechasse
114

HIGH TABLE
15 Les Ambassadeurs
147

BESPOKE GLAMOUR
16 Maison Calavas

GILDED SPLENDOUR
17 Église du Dôme

Hôtel des Invalides, 129, rue de Grenelle, 7th

Soaring over the gardens of Les Invalides and distinguished by its elongated cupola is one of Paris's greatest Baroque architectural wonders, designed by Jules Hardouin-Mansart in 1679 and completed in 1706. If the golden dome (regilded with 12 kilos of gold for the bicentennial of the French Revolution in 1989) doesn't lure you inside, then surely the prospect of seeing Napoleon's tomb will, despite the otherwise uncharismatic interior.

WINE TO START
18 Il Vino

13, boulevard de la Tour Maubourg, 7th

This menuless restaurant has turned out to be not such a crazy idea after all. The brainchild of Enrico Bernardo, Il Vino pairs food and wine in an unusual way: diners choose the wine, and then the chef decides what dish he will prepare. A South African white wine might be served with chestnut-flour spaghetti and clam sauce, and a Barbera d'Alba with *risotto con funghi porcini*. The bill will be sizeable, but you'll get to taste Salon Champagne or a Château d'Yquem. A wine bar? Sure, but a top-notch one.

FRIEND FROM THE SOUTH
19 L'Ami Jean

27, rue Malar, 7th

The straightforward statement on the sign outside – 'Cuisine basque' – is confirmed inside by the pepper braids and rugby paraphernalia hanging on the wall, both typical of southwest France. But you can expect far more from chef Stéphane Jégo than the local *piperade*, followed by ewe's milk cheese. Instead, he makes the most of seasonal produce in accordance with his regional origins, stuffing piquillo peppers with crab or serving black pudding in a salad. Connoisseurs will recognize a style of cooking reminiscent of La Régalade (p. 143), unsurprising given that Jégo trained there for several years.

SMALL BUT PERFECTLY FORMED
20 L'Astrance

FABLED FARE
21 Café Constant + Les Fables de la Fontaine

139 and 131, rue St-Dominique, 7th

With no less than three restaurants in rue St-Dominique, chef Christian Constant has become the key figure in the street's food scene. It all started a few years ago when he took over Violon d'Ingres, with Constant subsequently opening two more venues in cheaper and simpler style. The café is a true-to-form neighbourhood bistro, where you can sip a glass of wine at the counter while waiting to sit down to a rustic pâté or *quenelles de brochet*. A few steps further, Les Fables is rich in top-quality fish offerings.

ARTS OF OTHER CONTINENTS
22 Musée du Quai Branly

37, quai Branly, 7th

Designed by Jean Nouvel and opened by Jacques Chirac in 2006, the Musée du Quai Branly houses an extensive collection of arts from Africa, Oceania, Asia and the Americas. The new building is on a riverside site across from the Palais de Tokyo (p. 39), within walking distance from the Eiffel Tower and within sight of the Palais Chaillot. Unlike these historic edifices, however, this is a very modern (and controversial) addition to the city. The museum marks an effort to challenge 'the arrogance and ethnocentrism' of many European museums, but the spaces are more harmonious than combative, in a presentation that pays tribute to the 'art and civilization' of these non-European regions.

SCULPTURAL HOMAGE
23 Musée Bourdelle

16, rue Antoine Bourdelle, 15th

Emile Antoine Bourdelle worked as an assistant to Rodin, was a teacher of Giacometti and a contemporary of Maillol. Visitors to the city might know him by his muscular sculpture of Hercules the Archer, which is prominently on display in the Musée d'Orsay. Statues, paintings, sketches and works from Bourdelle's personal collection are set out in pleasant surroundings in the apartment and gardens that were once the sculptor's home and studio, with an extension by Christian de Portzamparc.

OLD-STYLE ELEGANCE
24 Le Dokhan's

This is a good place to have lunch after a visit to the Tour Eiffel – that is, if you're willing to whet your appetite on a twenty-minute walk. If so, you'll find yourself in a quiet neighbourhood, far away from all the tourist traps and hungry enough to enjoy Christian Etchebest's tempting cuisine. His weekly changing menu features modern Basque dishes, and might include roasted scallops in herbed butter or spring lamb from the Pyrenees served with white beans. To be savoured in very noisy but comfortingly warm surroundings.

One feels a little like a modern-day Alice in Wonderland here, encountering the allée formed by stepped concrete cubes, wrapped in box hedges, and leading to a tunnel of trees and beyond to other wonders, both formal and wild. Three-storey greenhouse towers on one side of a path are countered by small, shaded pergolas. A *jardin en mouvement* contains bamboo and other plants that rustle in a breeze, while other areas are planted by colour or form, all divided by geometric low stone walls and walks. Pavement fountains dance in front of the two great glassed conservatories. Landscape artists Gilles Clément and Alain Provost, along with architects, completed work in 1992 on former Citroën factory land.

If you claim to have any interest in the birth of modern design then a visit to this collection is a must, as it houses the complete notes on the life and work of one of the most influential architects of the 20th century. The Villa La Roche and Villa Jeanneret, both designed by the visionary architect, are home to Le Corbusier's drawings, plans and artworks, which he bequeathed on his death in 1965, with the aim of keeping them together as a comprehensive body of work. The Fondation has done just that, making the collection available to the public in its entirety, as well as holding periodic exhibitions. Furniture he designed alone and in collaboration with Pierre Jeanneret and Charlotte Perriand is also on display.

This new museum of architecture located in the east wing of the Palais de Chaillot is meant to be the largest of its kind in the world. Its three galleries, including a glass-roofed central gallery, cover some 8,000 square metres and chronicle over twelve centuries of French building design. The long gallery contains reproductions of architectural elements from the 11th to the 18th centuries, including decorative archways, medieval statuary, columns and entablatures; another gallery has wall paintings and stained-glass windows, including a copy of the great window at Chartres cathedral. A third gallery holds modern and contemporary examples, among them a reconstruction of an apartment designed by Le Corbusier.

The Musée d'Art Moderne already occupied one wing of the neoclassical Palais de Tokyo, built in 1937, but the need for 'flexible space in which to present international art' was the driving force behind the interior designed by Anne Lacaton and Jean-Philippe Vassal. And 'versatile' is certainly one word for it, and 'dynamic-industrial' are two more. Inside, the architects have created something akin to an open-plan artist's loft space by ripping out beams, floors and other obstructions to create a hangar-like backdrop for all size and manner of exhibitions, which are open from noon until midnight. Downstairs, the tabula rasa has been livened up in the colourful café area that spills out on to the terrace, where the hillside site becomes apparent and a view over the Seine is art of a different nature.

NOTES ON THE MASTER

33 Fondation Pierre Bergé, Yves St Laurent

5, avenue Marceau, 16th

Opposite the grand doors marked with the large 'YSL' is the entrance to the foundation's exhibition space and archives set up by Yves Saint Laurent's partner, Pierre Bergé. The main floor houses the public exhibition space, which has a programme that changes about twice a year. A recent exhibition focused on 'Théâtre, Cinema, Music-Hall, Ballet' and featured original fashion sketches and costumes. Upstairs a small bookshop has titles on YSL and fashion, and colourful postcards by the designer. Access to the 5,000 haute couture garments and 15,000 accessories in the archives on the 2nd and 3rd floors is by appointment.

SECOND-EMPIRE SOPHISTICATION

34 L'Hôtel de Sers

116

WINE-BAR CHIC

35 Les Caves Pétrissans

30 bis, avenue Niel, 17th

There are some wine bars where you bump into more Hermès ties than Nikes, and Les Caves Pétrissans, with its chic atmosphere and clientele, is one of them. But you'll never feel uncomfortable, since conviviality is this bistro's buzzword and people of all kinds rub shoulders around the bar. The décor is as ageless as the food – perfect home-cooking with set pieces of steak tartare, calf's head with shallot sauce, kidneys, to name a few. And since the place doubles as a vintner's, have a look at the remarkable wine list and then go next door and buy a bottle of your own.

ARTFUL BREADS

36 be boulangépicier

73, boulevard de Courcelles, 8th

Chef Alain Ducasse (see p. 147) has many more prominent venues for his culinary achievements, but this one, designed by Patrick Jouin and opened in conjunction with bread-master Eric Kayser, takes the humble dough to a higher plane. Along with a variety of golden loaves, sweet and savoury treats such as the triple *petits pains* (mini gourmet sandwiches on three kinds of bread) can be bought to take away or eaten in the stylish little café area, whose tables and chairs and even the wall mural in the loo tell you that this is more than just a baguette stop.

SIMPLY LUXURIOUS

37 Guy Savoy

134

SURPRISING DELIGHTS

38 Pierre Gagnaire

142

ELEGANCE WITHIN REACH

39 Le Chiberta

3, rue Arsène-Houssaye, 8th

This is a restaurant run by a three-starred chef without the matching prices. Recently taken over by Guy Savoy and entirely redecorated by architect Jean-Michel Wilmotte (see the MK2 Bibliothèque; p. 26), this venue is governed by the same spirit of natural elegance as the chef's more famous restaurant (p. 134). Skilled and friendly waiters dispatch simple yet thoroughly refined food. Favourite recipes include Bresse chicken terrine with foie gras seasoned with artichoke and truffle vinaigrette, spatchcocked pigeon with Espelette pepper (a Basque variety) or grapefruit terrine in Earl Grey sauce – none of which are necessarily cheap: you pay the price of being two steps away from the Champs-Élysées. The bar is perfect for sharing a whole rib of beef with a banker friend.

AUCTION-HOUSE EATERY

40 Artcurial Café

Hôtel Marcel Dassault,
7, rond-point des Champs-Élysées, 8th

Within the grand rooms of the Artcurial auction house premises of the Hôtel Marcel Dassault are a good bookshop and exhibition space, as well as a stylish little café designed by the Bouroullec brothers. On the busy rond-point, the café is a quiet little conservatory space with giant lampshades (orange and red), matte black tables and a steel floor adding a modern edge. The menu is very reasonable and offers fresh light dishes for lunch, such as savoury tarts, salads or an occasional chicken or fish *plat du jour*. Frequented by the auction house staff and visitors, it is open to the public, though a hidden gem.

GRAND PERFUMERIE AND SPA

41 Guerlain

166

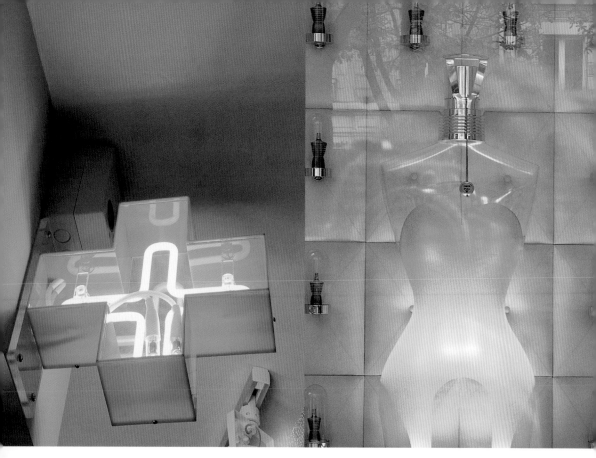

Publicis, founded in 1926, has been given a new face, a wavy steel and glass affair designed by American architect Michele Saee. Inside, it is part drugstore, part food hall and general store, all with grand style. The pharmacy is staffed by helpful, multi-lingual professionals, even on a Sunday. There is a glowing white bar and glass-enclosed brasserie serving a 'fast and good' thirty-minute menu developed by chef Alain Soulard, who worked under Alain Ducasse (see p. 147). There is also a cinema, two bookshops (with French and international books and magazines), beauty and designer concessions.

There was a time when he was considered something of a shock-monger. But today Gaultier is almost as fashion establishment as Dior. Thankfully, this doesn't mean that the former *enfant terrible* has mellowed too much. In 2002, the ever-active Gaultier settled into one of the princely avenues of the 8th arrondissement. The white padded walls and carved glass were designed by fellow Parisian Philippe Starck (see The Cristal Room; p. 146).

First opened in 1965, the Courrèges boutique of the 21st century has the space-age pure white and lucite décor that has both a futuristic and slightly retro feel, especially in the context of the go-go miniskirts, squared, above-the-knee shift dresses in window-pane checks, zippered white boots and bags, all looking slightly familiar but also very chic. Courrèges seems to have been suspended perfectly in time, except for the updated young shop assistants. Its pure aesthetic has the effect of making shoppers look like less-perfect intrusions. The Café Blanc next door is as shiny white and just as haughty.

Beef at three in the morning? Why should that sound eccentric? Especially if the meat comes straight from the Aubrac region, where the owner's family breeds this exquisite cattle. Many Parisian chefs know it and gather here after closing their own restaurants. Night owls, taxi drivers, lost tourists and beef worshippers know it, too, and the place is frequently overcrowded and the welcome may be less than wholehearted. If that should happen, call over a sommelier and let him help you find an absorbing bottle from the amazing wine list (900 references). Then sit back, relax and watch the sun rise.

Right Bank
Palais-Royal
Montorgueil

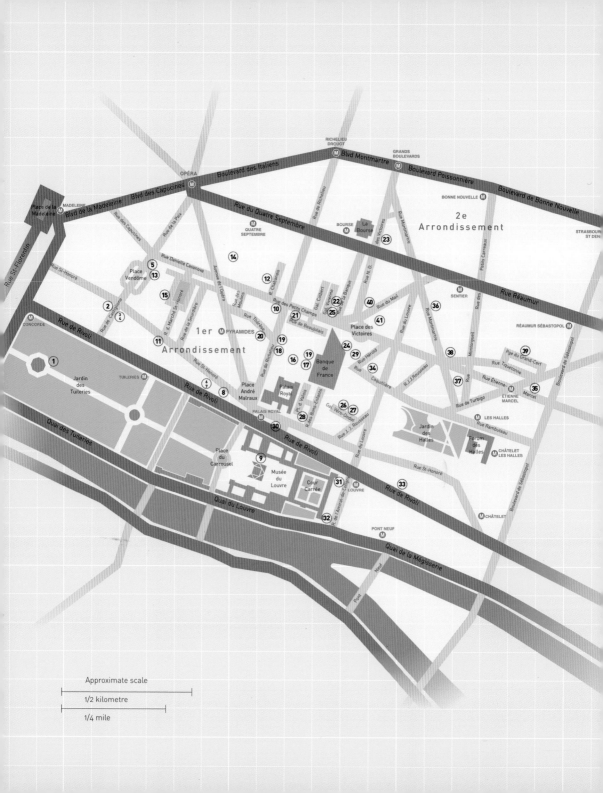

RICHELIEU
DROUOT

Ⓜ Blvd Montmartre

GRANDS
BOULEVARDS

OPÉRA

Boulevard des Italiens

Boulevard Poissonnière

Boulevard de Bonne Nouvelle

Blvd des Capucines

Ⓜ

BONNE NOUVELLE Ⓜ

2e
Arrondissement

MADELEINE Ⓜ

Blvd de la Madeleine

Rue du Quatre Septembre

Place de la
Madeleine

Rue des Capucines

Rue de la Paix

BOURSE
Ⓜ

La
Bourse

Rue Richelieu

Rue Montmartre

STRASBOURG
ST DEN

Rue St-Honoré

Rue St-Florentin

Rue Danielle Casanova

QUATRE
SEPTEMBRE

Ⓜ 73

Rue Réaumur

5

Place
Vendôme

13

Avenue de l'Opéra

14

Rue des Victoires

SENTIER
Ⓜ

RÉAUMUR SÉBASTOPOL Ⓜ

2

15

12

R. Chabanais

Gal. Colbert

Rue Vivienne

22

40

36

Rue du Mail

Rue des

Passage du Grand-Cerf

39

CONCORDE

Rue de Rivoli

Rue de Castiglione

10

Rue des Petits Champs

25

Rue de la Banque

38

Rue Étienne

Rue Montmartre

Marcel

35

1er

21

PYRAMIDES Ⓜ

Arrondissement

11

Rue Thérèse

20

18

19

Rue de Beaujolais

Place des
Victoires

41

R. J. J. Rousseau

Rue de Turbigo

ÉTIENNE
MARCEL

1

Jardin
des
Tuileries

TUILERIES Ⓜ

8

Place
André
Malraux

Rue St-Honoré

16

17

19

Banque
de France

24

29

34

Rue Hérold

Rue

Rue

Coquillière

37

LES HALLES Ⓜ

Quai des Tuileries

PALAIS ROYAL Ⓜ

Place
du
Carrousel

30

9

Palais
Royal

28

Pl. A. Malraux

Gal. Vero-Dodat

26

27

R. J. J. Rousseau

Rue du Louvre

Jardin
des
Halles

Rue Rambuteau

Forum
des
Halles

CHÂTELET
LES HALLES

Musée
du
Louvre

Cour
Carrée

31

LOUVRE Ⓜ

Rue de Rivoli

33

Rue St-Honoré

32

R. de l'Amiral de Coligny

CHÂTELET Ⓜ

Quai du Louvre

PONT NEUF

Quai de la Mégisserie

Approximate scale

1/2 kilometre

1/4 mile

The spiral of arrondissements, as conceived in the 19th century by urban planner extraordinaire Baron Haussmann, begins here, in the quarter dominated by the grand architectural spectacle of the Louvre, with the Louvre itself and the Jardin des Tuileries taking up most of the riverfront. This is still the heart of visitors' Paris, not as it was in the days when the Louvre was still a palace and Les Halles was a thriving marketplace, but a historic beating heart to which people are drawn for a glimpse of the Belle Époque and the *ancien régime*. When not held in thrall at the Louvre or the Musée des Arts Décoratifs (p. 49), people come here for star-quality shopping, eating and drinking. Some old and traditional, and some new and equally grand spots off the place Vendôme whisper to your pocketbook, as do the restaurants and bars, the oldest of which, Le Grand Véfour (p. 137), will take your breath away with its décor. Modern-day masters of grandeur, brothers Gilbert and Jean-Louis Costes, who ratcheted up the design of Parisian restaurant-bars with Café Costes (in collaboration with Philippe Starck) in 1984, created the stylish Café Marly (p. 49) overlooking I. M. Pei's glass pyramids at the Louvre and pulled out all the Empire stops at the Hôtel Costes (p. 158), brought to decadent life with the flamboyant design of Jacques Garcia.

A less modern extravagance is to be had in the *galeries*. These beautifully designed 19th-century covered passages were created to promote the fashionable Belle-Époque activity of shopping. Napoleon III's empress, Eugénie, led the nation, or at least the *nouveau riche*, in a taste for conspicuous consumption, which at the dawn of the 21st century has culminated in the birth of the 'concept store', where art, design and fashion meet to form a holistic experience. Shops like Colette (p. 49) pioneered the idea and design-leaders such as Comme des Garçons (p. 165) and established names like distinguished jewellers Van Cleef & Arpels (p. 162) have made just being inside the shop as important as the articles to be purchased.

The attempts to revive the fortunes of Les Halles, the centuries-old market, later enclosed by Napoleon III and replaced in the 1970s with a universally unloved complex, have not achieved continued success. Though the surrounding area is probably no less savoury than it has been for centuries, somehow the modern intrusion makes it that much more avoidable. But one only has to go a little farther north to the small pedestrianized streets of Montorgueil, around the rues Tiquetonne and Étienne-Marcel, to find cool and funky in a slightly more salubrious setting.

LES ARTS DÉCORATIFS

Musée Orang

1 Musée de l'Orangerie

Jardin des Tuileries, 1st

After a six-year renovation, the Orangerie was reopened in 2006 with a redesign by architect Olivier Brochet. The focus of the space is pointedly on Monet's *Les Nymphéas*, which were given to the museum by the artist on his death in 1926. The grand white ovoid spaces were designed specifically as Monet described to display the series that was inspired by a 'water garden' on his property at Giverny. Monet spent some thirty years recording the scenes there, and the eight panels on display represent 'the passing of the hours, from morning in the east to sunset in the west'. Light is filtered through large screened skylights, allowing a natural illumination without damaging the works. Stitched together, the great canvases extend six metres or longer. Downstairs, the collection of Walter and Paul Guillaume includes major works by Rousseau, Modigliani, Matisse, Cézanne, Renoir and Picasso.

SECOND-EMPIRE SEDUCTION

2 Hôtel Costes

158

SEXY STILETTOS

3 Rodolphe Menudier

169

BIJOUX PERFUME

4 JAR

164

CLASSIC MEN'S SHIRTS

5 Charvet

28, place Vendôme, 1st

'Trendy' is not a word you associate with this, one of Paris's last surviving traditional shirtmakers, but if you are looking for something with that quintessential Paris gentlemanly air, then this venerable old institution is a worthwhile stop. Made-to-measure shirts (still sewn one at a time in their workshop), as well as ties and handkerchiefs in dozens of fabrics and patterns and a selection of classic pyjamas and toiletries, are all on display in the reassuringly old-fashioned premises. The inventor of removable collars and cuffs, Charles Charvet opened up in 1838 and was soon shirtmaker to royalty and *nouveau riche* alike.

GRAND REOPENING

6 Musée des Arts Décoratifs

107, rue de Rivoli, 1st

Originally founded in 1882, the Musée des Arts Décoratifs grew out of the Universal Exhibitions as a way to promote the applied arts. After being closed for a ten-year renovation project, the museum reopened in 2006 with 150,000 objects dating from the Middle Ages to the present. The galleries were redesigned by a team of architects, with modern spatial and lighting features helping to highlight the vast collection on display. As part of the renovation, a large new museum shop, 107 Rivoli, was added, with several rooms of books, objets d'art, crafts, souvenirs and jewelry on display, as was the Saut du Loup restaurant and bar (p. 150).

SPLENDID SETTING

7 Le Saut du Loup

 150

AVANT-GARDE ANTIQUE

8 Astier de la Villatte

173, rue St-Honoré, 1st

At first glance, this shop looks quaintly old-fashioned with its creamy white ceramics and delicate glassware propped up on wooden shelves, but closer inspection reveals a distinctly modern edge. Inspired by 17th- and 18th-century tableware, the designs share the glossy white glaze and ornamental edges of antique models, but there are places where the earthenware peeks through the glaze and the shape is slightly askew. The old shop also keeps its antique, slightly worn persona as well, making an inviting backdrop for this charmingly quirky collection of ceramics, glassware, candles, furniture and assorted other items.

MUSEUM OPULENCE

9 Le Café Marly

Palais du Louvre, 93, rue de Rivoli, 1st

Some say you cannot get a feel for Paris without sitting at least once on the terrace of the Café Marly, facing I.M. Pei's beautiful glass pyramids at the Musée du Louvre. There is a lot to see while you sip a coffee: models, Gucci worshippers, actors you haven't yet heard of, armchairs designed by Olivier Gagnère. The Marly is one of the Costes brothers' major successes of the 1990s. Knowing that, you should not complain about the fashion food (chicken with Thai basil, gazpacho, duck *brochettes* with caramel and coconut), nor the prices.

You might not want to come to Paris to meet English-speaking tourists, but what you might want to find is a wily wine bar – even if it's run by a Scot called Tim Johnston. Therefore, seize the opportunity to ask the owner (in English, obviously) what's worth looking at from the French vineyards. He might have you start with a glass of Purple Four (a Rhône valley vintage specially blended for him), then take you to the Barossa valley (the international wine list is clever, though a bit expensive). Meanwhile, you'll be pecking at some nice tapas – hot chorizo included – or cheese plates. Wine can also be purchased to take home.

The woman who created this early 'concept store', mixing art and fashion and related books in a high-design backdrop, did it fashionably on a first-name basis. Now when such holistic blends have become much more commonplace, Colette still holds the reins with this original and enduringly top-notch fashion emporium. The three floors of minimally designed premises feature an international collection of clothing and accessories, art objects, electronic gadgetry and cosmetics from the pantheon of designers. Downstairs everything from furniture to toiletries is on offer, as well as a restaurant and the famed 'water bar', where you can sample from around eighty brands from all over the globe. Despite its high profile, this is a shop where browsing is part of the experience, with a photo gallery and bookshop on the mezzanine level, as well as space for exhibitions.

Lampshades, rugs and accessories made from woven pineapple fibres, nettles and water hyacinths are just some of the unusual delights that Corinne Muller and Marianne Oudin stock in their popular and highly eco-friendly shop. A whole range of different plant fibres are used by the designers to create unusual textiles, which they dye themselves to achieve objects and fabrics of startling and startlingly natural beauty. You can also order their fabrics in lengths, for your own upholstery, shades or wall coverings. They've become a favourite of modern designers looking for a distinctive natural texture and vivid hues.

Call it unfair if you wish, but *c'est la vie*: until quite recently, Drouant was classified in the not-very-glamorous category of restaurants where nothing ever happened (except perhaps once a year, during the Prix Goncourt celebrations). But since the arrival of the Westermann-Clemot duet (already known from Mon Vieil Ami; p. 85), the place has had more of a buzz. But don't expect a revolution: no dancing on tables, no coat of pink paint on the Ruhlmann ironwork banister, no other atmosphere than that of a trendy brasserie, with classic daily specials (such as *bouchée à la reine*) next to more innovative dishes (Thai-style beef).

16 Les Jardins du Palais-Royal
between rue de Montpensier and rue de Valois, 1st

This beautifully secluded garden is the kind of place you
hate to tell many people about for fear of letting the secret
out. At one end is a paved courtyard that often features
sculptural displays, and is a magnet for children in the
afternoon, who are often to be seen playing around the
objets d'art. Most of the rectangular courtyard is filled
with espaliered trees and formal flower-beds, gravel walks,
benches and a gentle fountain. The surrounding cafés
have different opening hours, but the updated Villa Lys
is usually a good bet for a table outside in the afternoon.
Otherwise just find a bench under the trees and soak
up some peaceful Parisian atmosphere.

SHOES FROM THE CATWALK
17 Pierre Hardy

THE WHITE ROOMS
18 Martin Margiela
25 bis, rue de Montpensier, 1st

Situated on a quiet street alongside the Palais-Royal and
somewhat sequestered, Martin Margiela's shop is bursting
with creative energy inside. Two floors of stark interiors
float behind the black-painted frontage. T-shirts, jumpers
and accessories are arranged in tidy colourful bundles
in honeycombs of white shelving on the ground floor,
while a video screen at the back provides techno-fashion
ambience. Upstairs is the larger, more formal collection.
Margiela made his name after working with Jean Paul
Gaultier (pp. 42 and 54) in the 1980s, and his creations still
have a highly inventive edge.

LITTLE BLACK DRESSES
19 Didier Ludot
20–24, galerie de Montpensier (vintage) and 125, galerie
de Valois (La Petite Robe Noire), 1st

Fashion stylist Didier Ludot has been drawing celebrities
and film and TV costume directors to his overflowing
rooms of vintage haute couture at nos 20-24 for years.
More recently he has focused a particular fashion obsession
and opened a second shop across the Jardins du Palais-
Royal in the galerie de Valois, an homage to *la petite robe
noire* at no. 125. These sexy designer numbers from past and
present confirm that there will never be anything quite like
the little black dress.

BOIS & FORÊTS
Christian Astuguevieille

BOXING CLEVER
20 Claude Jeantet
10, rue Thérèse, 1st

Though most of her creations were never boxes, architect Claude Jeantet's cardboard curiosities have that appeal of humble materials being put to somewhat loftier use. Delightful dogs, cats, rabbits and crocodiles appear alongside useful household items like picture frames and copies of the artist's book on how to do it yourself with cardboard. She has expanded her range to include furniture, corner units and stools, and uses other base materials as well, like sponge. All in this enchanting little container of a shop.

TIMELESS PLEASURE
21 Le Grand Véfour
137

POSH PROMENADE
22 Galerie Vivienne
4, rue des Petits-Champs and 6, rue Vivienne, 2nd
• Jean Paul Gaultier, no. 6
• A Priori Thé, nos 35–37
• Christian Astuguevieille, no. 42

Parisian covered passages are a delight, particularly on a rainy day. But the 19th-century Galerie Vivienne offers a lavish sort of shopping and shelter. The grand arcade is home to one of Jean Paul Gaultier's retail spaces (see also p. 42), some fine stalls of books and prints and the lovely A Priori Thé for afternoon refreshment. At no. 42, artist, designer and fragrance advisor to Comme des Garçons, Christian Astuguevieille, has an outlet for his furniture, as well as his sculpture and pen-and-ink drawings.

LOCAL ASSETS
23 Gallopin
137

Two steps away from the place des Victoires and its über-trendy fashion stores, this unconspicuous-looking bistro looks quite lonely. But the executives from the nearby Banque de France and local fashionistas must have elected it as their headquarters for a good reason. Indeed, the chalkboard shows a superior wine list, paired with high-level bistro dishes, prepared from the best products. Mackerels in coriander jelly, veal carpaccio with Parmesan cheese, copious beef tartare, squab with chitterling sausage, all to be savoured after a mandatory appetizer of Auvergne and Spanish cured meats – because *fines gueules* means 'discerning foodies'.

Like many Parisian *galeries*, this covered passage was something of a precursor to a modern mall but much more picturesque. The Galerie du Passage, run by Pierre Passbon, is a highlight. Specializing in French furnishings of the the 20th century, he counts Alexandre Noll, Jean-Michel Franck and Christian Bérard among his collection. He also hosts exhibitions of design and photography, including the recent 'Fetish' by David Lynch, featuring shoes by Christian Louboutin (p. 169). Cosmetics can be individually mixed at one of three outlets run by former YSL director Terry de Gunzburg, aptly named 'By Terry'.

Cheverny Blanc
Macon Blanc
• VOUVRAY
• POUILLY FUISSÉ
• LOUPIAC
• CHIROUBLES
Côtes de Brouilly
• RÉGNIÉ
• Fleurie
Juliénas
DOMAINE DE SAINTE-ROSE
    (VIN DE PAYS D'OC)
Bordeaux
• COSTIÈRES DE NÎMES
• CROZES-HERMITAGE
Chinon
• FAUGÈRES (Langue Doc)

• LADOIX ROUGE
• SAVIGNY LES BEAUNE

• Nos vins sont m
Bouteilles par le

28 Galerie Patrick Fourtin

9, rue des Bons-Enfants, 1st

Selling mostly furniture and objects from the 1930s, '40s and '50s, Patrick Fourtin has made a name for himself as a purveyor of modern French design. His favoured creators include André Arbus, Gilbert Poillerat, Jacques Adnet and Rollin. 'Occasionally we will have something from the 19th century,' says co-gallerist Roberto Ardone, 'perhaps a great Italian mirror, to show that you can have a space that is not fixed in a particular period.' They also try to arrange the gallery 'as if it were a private house', with a mixture of styles and periods; the shop also occasionally hosts exhibitions. As the French 1940s hot up for collectors, Patrick Fourtin is all aglow.

A LITTLE ROMANCE
29 Sandrine Philippe

6, rue Hérold, 1st

In an area of flashy designs and even flashier retail spaces, it is refreshing to find such understated glamour. 'I make clothes with a story, a history,' says the soft-spoken young designer who worked for the house of Courrèges (p. 43) before starting her own label in 1997. She aims for designs that are 'poetic and feminine'. Using the cottons, silks and wools that she then customizes with 'dyeing, burning, painting and artisanal applications', her clothes are uniquely soft, romantic and sophisticated. The shop reflects a marriage of romance and cool aesthetic, its concrete floor set off with recessed flowers and violet walls hung with delicate jewelry. Her approach is the opposite of shock value: 'I want customers to feel something with these garments,' Philippe explains, 'like they have always known them.'

CAPITAL ANTIQUES
30 Le Louvre des Antiquaires

2, place du Palais-Royal, 1st

Originally founded in 1855 by Messrs Chauchard and Hériot as the Grands Magasins du Louvre, it was the first shop of its kind in Paris. Today 250 dealers are arranged on three levels across the rue de Rivoli from the Louvre. Because dealers sign an agreement to respect certain rules regarding the age and quality of their objects, they are subject to quality-control checks by experts, thus ensuring that the standards are high and the dealers are reputable. It might not fit everyone's pocketbook, but you can always bargain, especially if you're paying in cash.

LITERARY BAR
31 Le Fumoir

MAKING SCENTS
32 La Grande Boutique de L'Artisan Parfumeur

2, rue l'Amiral-de-Coligny, 1st

The flagship store of the perfume empire, which was started in 1976 by Jean Laporte but is now owned by an American company, retains a sense of grand Parisian style and specialist status. In addition to the numerous brands on offer, there are around thirty fragrances sold under the Artisan label and a personal fragrance-combining service available for those willing to seriously splash out on olfactory finery. Not content with merely selling the stuff, the store offers evening lectures on the art, science and history of perfumery. They also stock room fragrances, creams, candles and even scents to keep your car smelling heavenly.

STREET-STYLE CHIC
33 Surface to Air

46, rue l'Arbre-Sec, 1st

Set among the well-established upmarket brands near the Louvre, this boutique-cum-gallery in a grafitti-sprayed loft space takes the concept store to its nouvelle-punk conclusion, with clothes by lesser-known avant-garde designers, along with their own label track suits and T-shirts, dresses, jewelry and accessories by various creators. The product of seven young art-design entrepreneurs, Surface to Air is also the headquarters of their photography and fashion company.

CHEAP AND VERY CHEERFUL
34 La Cloche des Halles

28, rue Coquillière, 1st

It's best to avoid this funny little bistro at lunchtime, when local workers pour in to occupy the tiny tables. But this is one of the best cheap bites in the neighbourhood, and a classic wine bar of Les Halles since many a year (the owner, Serge Lesage, still bottles his fine Beaujolais himself). Farm cheeses are perfect (don't miss the Cantal), as well as all the pork classics (white and country ham, *jambon persillé* with its parsley aspic, and many varieties of sausages). Just like going back to the 1950s.

35 Declercq Passementiers
15, rue Étienne-Marcel, 1st

If the French had the patent on dramatic period interiors, then the early part of this century has confirmed that they intend to keep up the trend, as seen in the layering of rich fabrics and patterns à la Jacques Garcia (see Hôtel Costes; p. 158) and Olivier Gagnère (see 15cent15; p. 151). It makes sense then that such designers would have places like this where they can stock up on some of the key ingredients for embellishing a hem, say, gathering a swag, or tying off a grand drapery in true Parisian style.

36 Librairie Gourmande
90, rue Montmartre, 2nd

The cooks' favourite bookshop has relocated to larger premises from St-Germain-des-Prés and still keeps a comprehensive stock of books on everything from 'the art of the table' to titles on the history of cooking to books on French regional and world cuisines, as well as cocktail recipes and tomes on wine. Find books by Alain Ducasse (see p. 147), Jamie Oliver, Michel Roux, Kristof Coppens and Charlie Trotter, among hundreds of others with a substantial number of titles in English and other languages.

37 Spa Nuxe
32, rue Montorgueil, 1st

Aliza Jabes, photogenic president of Nuxe cosmetics company, and celebrity hair stylist John Nollet have created one of the French capital's more atmospheric spa and beauty centres within the medieval stone walls of a building near Les Halles. Off the narrow street, through a glass-filled stone arch, dusky-scented, candlelit rooms for massage, hammam, hair and beauty treatments are tucked away in a haven of insulated calm. The wood-beamed rooms hung with lengths of white fabric and dotted with exotic flowers ooze quiet serenity. An indoor river flows through the Turkish bath area, which is also lapped by reflecting pools.Treatments are available for men and women and feature Nuxe natural products, of course, and range from manicures to the soin rêverie Orientale body treatment with hammam, full body scrub, purifying Rassoul wrapping and massage. Booking is sometimes necessary three months in advance.

38 Kiliwatch
64, rue Tiquetonne, 2nd

Rue Tiquetonne is a narrow street filled with boutiques, little restaurants and workshops, all cheek-by-jowl and all full of youthful vibrancy. Kiliwatch presents designer and second-hand street fashions, having begun as a 'Kilo-shop', where second-hand clothes are sold by the kilo. This outlet has been around for over ten years and its popularity only seems to increase. There are jeans, tops and sport shoes from an international roster of street-fashion designers from Diesel and Pépé to Swedish line Redwood, sixty in all to choose from.

39 Passage du Grand-Cerf
- La Corbeille, no. 5, 2nd
- As'Art, no. 3, 2nd

The pretty wrought-ironwork of this unusually tall, light-filled passage, built around 1835, is only part of its charm. Running between rue St-Denis and rue Dussoubs, and parallel to the small, design-filled rue Tiquetonne, the Passage du Grand Cerf provides a Belle-Époque setting for modern design flair and funky fashion accessories. La Corbeille is a haven for finds from the 1950s to the present. Pierre Paulin, Charles and Ray Eames, Eero Saarinen and Olivier Mourgue stand proud as the classics that they are among a host of objects and lighting that is slightly more whimsical but never tacky. As'Art also presents ethnic and African pieces made by contemporary designers.

40 Chez Georges
135

41 Deuce
7, rue d'Aboukir, 2nd

They began by making finely crafted leather goods and accessories (such as a chessboard in multi-coloured pieces and made-to-order calfskin backgammon sets) that gained the attention of some high-profile fans in France and the US, but Isabelle Guédon and Benjamin Caron recently refurbished and restarted their shop with forays into woodworking. They continue to produce pieces of skilled craftsmanship. Their little shop and studio off the rue Étienne-Marcel showcases their full, detail-driven range.

Grands Boulevards
Pigalle
Montmartre

Place des Abbesses (inset)

ABBESSES
Rue Yvonne-le-Tac
Rue Tardieu
Place St-Pierre
Rue des Abbesses
d'Orsel
19 25 26 29
Rue de Steinkerque
Rue des Martyrs
16 17
18
27
28
Place Charles-Dullin
Rue d'Orsel
Rue Dancourt
ANVERS
14
Boulevard de Clichy
Boulevard de Rochechouart

Porte de St-Ouen
Porte de Clignancourt
33

Boulevard Ney

PORTE DE ST OUEN
PORTE DE CLIGNANCOURT
Rue Championnet
Rue Championnet
SIMPLON

18e Arrondissement

GUY MÔQUET

Avenue de St-Ouen

JULES JOFFRIN

LAMARCK CAULAINCOURT
Rue Caulaincourt
Rue Custine

LA FOURCHE

Cimetière de Montmartre

24

Basilique du Sacré Coeur

Rue Caulaincourt

21 20
R. Ravignan
R. Houdon
22 23
Rue des Abbesses
Rue des Trois Frères
34
BARBÈS ROCHECHOUART

Boulevard BLANCHE
de Clichy
Rue Fontaine

Musée de la Vie Romantique

PLACE DE CLICHY

ABBESSES
Rue Y. le Tac
Pl St-Pierre
R. des Martyrs
Rue d'Orsel
ANVERS
PIGALLE
Rue Lepic
Boulevard de
Rochechouart

15
Rue Chaptal

9e Arrondissement

13
Avenue Trudaine

ROME
Boulevard des Batignolles

VILLIERS

MONCEAU
Boulevard de Courcelles

Parc de Monceau

COURCELLES

2
Musée Nissim de Camondo

8e Arrondissement

Rue de Parme

LIÈGE

EUROPE

Rue d'Amsterdam

Rue de Clichy

Rue Blanche

Rue de la Rochefoucauld

SAINT GEORGES
Rue N.D. de Lorette
10
12
Rue des Martyrs
Rue Milton
11

Musée Gustave Moreau
9 8 7
Rue St Lazare

Rue de la Chaussée d'Antin

TRINITÉ
Rue de Châteaudun

N.D. DE LORETTE
LE PELETIER

Rue la Fayette
Rue Drouot
Rue le Peletier
Rue de Maubourge
Lamartine
CADET
Rue la Fayette
6

Rue de Monceau

Musée Jacquemart André
1
Boulevard Haussmann

Boulevard Haussmann

ST LAZARE
Rue St

Lazare

HAVRE CAUMARTIN

4
Rue Tronchet

CHAUSSÉE D'ANTIN
AUBER

OPÉRA

Place de la Madeleine

Bd de la Madeleine
Bd des Capucines

d'Antin

Bd des Italiens

RICHELIEU DROUOT

5
R. du Fbg Montmartre
R. du Faubourg Poissonnière
Rue Richer
GRANDS BOULEVARDS
Bd Montmartre

BONNE NOUVELLE

Av. Michelet

Approximate scale

1 kilometre

1/2 mile

The great thoroughfares were first laid out as tree-lined avenues by Louis XIV and widened to Empire proportions by Napoleon III's urban modernizer, Baron Haussmann, in the 19th century. Despite periods of neglect those grand boulevards, lined as they are by great houses, maintain the poise of an area that was then the height of fashion. Around the same time, the 9th arrondissement was dubbed the 'Nouvelle-Athènes', taking its name from both the area's neoclassical buildings and from the group of artists and writers who converged in literary and artistic salons here. The Musée de la Vie Romantique (p. 68) provides an atmospheric snapshot of the creative period peopled by such characters as Eugène Delacroix, Frédéric Chopin and George Sand, as does another artistic house-museum, the Musée Gustave Moreau (p. 67). Though many streets are now unremarkable, the grandeur epitomized by the boulevards and the extravagant Second Empire Opéra Garnier still exists in pockets around the 9th, as does a certain subtle artistic flavour. Pigalle, another formerly artistic neighbourhood, is experiencing something of a renaissance with a new arty hotel (see Hôtel Amour; p. 122) and café revival around the place George Toudouze and the rue des Martyrs (p. 67), known today more for its mix of new and bohemian fashions than for its sacrificial history.

La butte, as it is known to Parisians, meaning the 'hill' or 'mound', refers to the place where St Denis was decapitated by Romans in the 3rd century. It was later called Mons Martyrum, which evolved to Montmartre. By the 19th century, as Haussmann ploughed through the heart of Paris, Montmartre remained a village idyll, with thatched cottages, windmills (*moulins*) and vineyards. Artists Renoir, Braque, Van Gogh, Dufy and Toulouse-Lautrec began filing in to the preserved rural corner. Utrillo was a native and painted some of the most evocative scenes of his home turf, but it was Toulouse-Lautrec's tributes to the great Moulin Rouge, which opened in 1889, and its musical stars like Jane Avril that put Montmartre on the tourist map. Today, artistic creativity is once again booming in Montmartre, but not in the 'artist'-filled place du Tertre. Boutiques selling everything from antiques to hand-made jewelry to modern furniture and new designs, as well as art galleries, are flourishing around the rue des Abbesses, rue Durantin, place Charles-Dullin (p. 72) and the newly reinvigorated rue des Gardes (p. 73). The best bars, pubs and cafés are those that manage to preserve some of the historic and romantic associations together with a modern attitude. Now the old quarter has a hotel (see L'Hôtel Particulier; p. 118) that celebrates both its artistic heritage and elysian charms in true style.

1 Musée Jacquemart André
158, boulevard Haussmann, 8th

Their subtitle is 'the most sumptuous residence in Paris' and it's not all hyperbole, though it is rather overwhelming. Edouard André was head of a great banking family and already an art collector when he met Nélie Jacquemart, who was commissioned to paint his portrait. Together they amassed a collection of works by some of the world's best-known artists and exhibited them in their exquisitely decorated mansion, built in 1875. The many rooms are kept generally as they were before Nélie died and bequeathed the collection to the state in 1913, but as the couple's tastes ran to historic opulence, so does the museum today. Many rooms are spectacular in their own right, but together they make for an astounding display of grandeur. Works by David, Boucher, Chardin and Fragonard are among the treasures in the French collection. The pair also had a great fondness for Italian and Dutch painting, and tapestries, furniture and objects in the private and grand 'informal' apartments are displayed in stunning Louis XV and Empire settings. The spectacular tea room, a destination in its own right, is housed in the former dining room, which is draped in red velvet and Brussels tapestries and boasts a ceiling painted by Tiepolo.

THE PETIT TRIANON IN PARIS
2 Musée Nissim de Camondo
63, rue de Monceau, 8th

For a museum whose treasures came from a family that knew such tragedy, the Musée Nissim de Camondo is surprisingly exuberant, a celebration of 18th-century French decorative arts and craftsmanship. Jacob, Sèvres, Meissen, Huet and a host of other names linked to the golden age of French decoration fill the meticulously laid-out rooms. The banking family de Camondo were known as 'the Rothschilds of the East', coming from Constantinople to establish branches in Paris. Moïse de Camondo tore down the family house on this site in 1910 and had a new building erected, inspired by the Petit Trianon at Versailles. The museum is named for his son, Nissim, who was killed in the First World War. His daughter, Béatrice, was later deported by the Nazis along with her husband and children and died at Auschwitz.

ART AND CUISINE NOUVEAU
3 Senderens
140

GRAND MAGASIN DINING
4 Brasserie Printemps
Printemps de la Mode, 6th floor, 9th

For several years now, Parisian department stores have been competing not only with their fashion concessions and layouts, but also with their eating and drinking venues. While the Bon Marché (p. 163) has Delicabar (p. 33), Printemps has created a string of stylish food stops across its three buildings (Homme, Maison and Mode), including the Biotifull Café, by the people behind the former R'Aliment in the Marais, a concession of Alain Ducasse's be boulangépicier (p. 40), as well as a sprawling formal dining room under the stained-glass Art Nouveau dome on the sixth floor of the Women's Store. Designer Didier Gomez revamped the whole room by introducing vivid red walls around the periphery, a bright yellow lighted bar, and a giant ball pendant hanging from the centre of the dome. There is also a Ladurée trolley on the first floor and a World Bar, designed by Paul Smith, on the fifth floor of the Men's Store.

TREATS FOR THE WHOLE FAMILY
5 La Mère de Famille
35, rue du Faubourg-Montmartre, 9th

Another stop on the Drouot route (around the famous auction houses), this beautiful old-fashioned shopfront shows a date of 1761, but the interior is wonderfully 19th century, selling biscuits, chocolates and cordials in the lovely packaging that the French bestow on little luxuries, and sweets in gleaming glass jars. The paintwork is slightly more worn than you'll find in the grander shops of the Marais or St-Germain-des-Prés, but, as the name suggests, the atmosphere is also that much more comforting.

FANTASTIC FOOTWEAR
6 Karine Arabian
4, rue Papillon, 9th

Former head of design for Chanel, Karine Arabian, now sells her own range of colourful shoes, bags and accessories on a triangular corner site, which is like a stylish oasis in this rather less interesting part of the 9th. Bold in hues and studded with beads or rhinestones, her shoes have a slight 1940s look, but with a hint of sexy extravagance. The 2007 range was all shiny patent leather, spat-style ankle boots and black or burgundy pumps with square heels. The shop itself pays homage to the Art Déco period, featuring pieces collected by the designer.

7 Chez Jean
8, rue St-Lazare, 9th

Nowadays talented and ambitious restaurateurs wouldn't even think of taking up business anywhere else than on the Left Bank. Yet Frédéric Guidoni, ex-maître d' at the famous Taillevent, has made a striking début with this wood-panelled brasserie near the rue des Martyrs (see right). And chef Benoît Bordier proves an imaginative young recruit. His snail and asparagus monkfish with rosemary lettuce, confit of free-range pork with carrots and cocoa-lychee-red grapefruit milkshake are definitely worth crossing the Seine for. The wine list, too, bears absolutely no reproach.

SERIOUS BEAUTY PRODUCTS
8 Detaille
10, rue St-Lazare, 9th

The cosmetics line started in 1910 with a face cream made for women riding in the first automobiles, who had to deal with open-air conditions and plagues of dust. Madame Detaille, for whom the cream was made, went on to market it from her home, along with a growing selection of new products that are still seen by many women as beauty essentials, like the all-natural rice powder in pure white and other tones.

HOUSE OF ART
9 Musée Gustave Moreau
14, rue de La Rochefoucauld, 9th

Born in Paris in 1826, Gustave Moreau was a prolific painter who helped to usher in the Symbolist and Surrealist movements. Moreau intended that the house and studio where he worked with such great intensity should be preserved as a museum to 'give a small idea of the person I was and the atmosphere in which I liked to dream'. Thousands of works, from delicate sketches of animals and plants to monumental canvases depicting scenes from the Bible, myth and fantasy are displayed in two large, light-filled studio rooms joined by an iron spiral staircase. Domestic rooms, including one devoted to his student and mistress, present an intriguing glimpse of late-19th-century French bourgeois life.

ARTHOUSE ROMANCE
10 Hôtel Amour
122

SMALL PLEASURES
11 Spring
28, rue de la Tour d'Auvergne, 9th

His name is Daniel Rose and he has heard the American-in-Paris stuff a thousand times. There may be a good reason for that, though: like Gene Kelly in the movie, he's got rhythm! And he sure needs it to feed sixteen guests every night in his tiny, 16-square-metre restaurant. Standing behind the counter that separates the open kitchen from the dining-room, this young Chicago-born chef prepares a unique, four-course menu in carefully thought-through neoclassical style. If you're lucky, you might taste his fantastic roast squab served with the smoothest, silkiest cauliflower and almond purée, or his foie gras with beetroot. Then you will understand why there is such a long queue to get in (savvy diners book two weeks in advance).

BAKERS AND BOLD DESIGNS
12 Rue des Martyrs
- Arnaud Delmontel, no. 39, 9th
- Rose Bakery, no. 46, 9th
- Emmanuelle Zysman, no. 81, 18th
- Heaven, no. 83, 18th

No longer a route of painful pilgrimage, the rue des Martyrs is a march of buzzing cafés and independent shops that offer creative substance and sustenance on the climb toward the *butte* of Montmartre. Beginning with the corner of rue Navarin, just along from the funky new-art gatherings of the Hôtel Amour (p. 122), the *patisserie* Arnaud Delmontel has entered the history books, winning the award for 'best baguette in Paris 2007', a title he proudly displays in the window. He's also known for his assortment of pastries, including exquisite lemon puffs and almond croissants. Across the road at no. 46, husband-and-wife team Jean-Charles (who set up the successful French-style restaurant and café Villandry in London) and Rose Carrarini (who is English) have gone back to modest beginnings, with little tables and chairs in a rustic cavernous space selling organic salads, soups, quiches and baked goods. (Rose's book *Breakfast Lunch Tea* is available at the Librairie Gourmande; p. 58). Farther up the road, past the avenue Trudaine, the creative boutiques begin popping up. Emmanuelle Zysman has had a shop on this parade for several years now, and people keep coming back for her collections of new French designers. A few doors up at Heaven, Lee-Anne Wallis sells her own designs for men and women that keep a modern edge to easygoing fabrics and shapes.

13 Et puis c'est tout
72, rue des Martyrs, 18th

As the rue des Martyrs (see also p. 67) marches up towards the increasingly trendy and craft-filled lanes of Montmartre, this small gallery of modern and retro furnishings, lighting and objects is bound to distract you from your walk. It is not the streamlined mid-century tables, chairs, desks and lamps that are the most striking (though there are some fine pieces), but the other side of the creative world, the collections of branded items, such as glasses, ashtrays and serving trays stamped with vintage French product trademarks that really catch the eye. Vincent Venen, who runs the shop along with his wife, Michèle, buys internationally but specializes in French designs from the 1950s, '60s and '70s.

ARTY BAR
14 La Fourmi Café
74, rue des Martyrs, 18th

La Fourmi is a bar oozing with bohemian characters, who come to drink beneath its wine-bottle chandelier before heading off to neighbourhood gigs, such as the world music on stage at Le Divan du Monde across the road. From heavily pierced goths in white face paint and black gear to flannel-shirted loungers whose tastes are probably more of the metal variety, the crowd at La Fourmi is a good cross-section of clubbers, night owls and casual drinkers. During the day it's a casual café where people come for a coffee or a snack and to read the paper.

NOTES FROM THE 'NEW ATHENS'
15 Musée de la Vie Romantique
Hôtel Scheffer-Renan, 16, rue Chaptal, 9th

This museum is not about love or even love letters, but is mostly filled with objects and furniture belonging to George Sand. It was Ary Scheffer, however, court painter to Louis Philippe, who actually lived in the house and ran a salon, which was attended by such luminaries as Frédéric Chopin, Eugène Delacroix, Jean-Auguste Ingres, Franz Liszt and Gustave Moreau (whose own house was turned into a museum; p. 67), as well as Chopin's lover, Sand. It is the period more than the art that is celebrated here, a time when the area was known as the 'Nouvelle-Athènes' because of the high concentration of artistic-philosophical minds and a certain modern spirit of enlightenment that they represented.

16 Pamp'lune

4 bis, rue Piémontési, 18th

Beautifully made, wonderfully detailed children's clothing, stitched on the premises by Valerie Perrin and Evelyne Brunot, who worked as designers for the Bon Marché (p. 163) before opening their boutique for 0-to-10-year-olds. The bright painted front signals the rich array of colours and textures inside as Perrin and Brunot prefer a bit of funky over traditional cuts and colours. Wide-wale corduroy trousers for boys have colourful trim details on the waist and pockets. Girls' dresses have bold patterns and deep hues, and all fabrics are pleasingly robust.

FUTURE COUTURE

17 FuturWare Lab

2, rue Piémontési, 18th

Russian designer Tatiana Lebedev moved to Paris in 1990 and set up her own label in 1997. Her taste is 'architectural, inspired by the Russian Constructivist style of the early 20th century'. Yet by employing soft fabrics like cashmere, flannel and silk in warm colours, she makes architecture not only wearable but also highly desirable. Sharply angled and smooth-fitting T-shirts and crisp denim skirts, as well as similar lines in leather or grey felt, have a definite futuristic look, but appear sensual rather than silly. As the name of the boutique suggests, Lebedev is also a purveyor of new technologies, so expect some unusual materials, as well as innovative cuts and combinations.

BRIGHT AND BEAUTIFUL

18 Patricia Louisor

16, rue Houdon, 18th

On a street known mainly for the fashion of its local transvestites, young and talented Patricia Louisor set up her small, vividly wrapped shop in 1991, making use of the vast fabric emporium of the nearby Marché St-Pierre to create her designs of 'simplicity and originality'. Her well-priced clothes 'for working, dancing or seduction' soon brought her notoriety, mainly by word of mouth. Today, she is a featured designer among the artisans of Montmartre, with a collection that is sexy with substance. Using plush fabrics cut on the bias, wrapped close to the body and flared at the wrist or ankle, she aims to create comfort of movement 'without sacrificing femininity and without adhering to the dictates of the latest fashion'.

CONCRETE WONDER
19 Église St-Jean-de-Montmartre
19, rue des Abbesses, 18th

The place des Abbesses is a picturesque spot, not only for its Hector Guimard Métro entrance but also for its pioneering *fin-de-siècle* church. Completed in 1904 to a design by Anatole de Baudot, former assistant to architectural visionary Eugène-Emmanuel Viollet-le-Duc, it is one of the first examples in Europe of reinforced concrete used for its sculptural qualities – a thrilling and innovative reinterpretation of the Gothic vault.

COOL COLLECTIVE
20 Fanche et Flo
19, rue Durantin, 18th

Fanche and Flo have been pushing the boundaries of fashion since they met after studying at the Sorbonne. Their clothing features bold combinations of colour, pattern and texture: a T-shirt with a bright square of fabric and zip across the front, swatches of neon or contrasts of stripy knits. Together with their three partners they have formed Sirop de Paris, designing avant-garde textiles, lighting, jewelry and furnishings, and making their little shop in Montmartre a bright and varied beacon of creativity. Some 'fetish' items include the 'Barbie skirt', the 'sock-pot', the 'minimal bag' and the 'bookshop flowerpot'. See for yourself.

ETHNIC UNDERGROUND
21 Le Doudingue
24, rue Durantin, 18th

Le Doudingue stands out among the drinking spots of Montmartre for its distinctive interior, derived from 'a mix of Baroque and Oriental, Parisian flea market and objects from India and Iran'. Opened by owner-manager Afshin Assadian with his wife, Valérie, and friend Jimmy Fofana in 2002, Doudingue ('crazy but nice') was the trio's attempt to move from large club venues to the more intimate atmosphere of a bar and restaurant. DJs still spin records, but the plush bar area is good for a glass of wine or a tropical drink following an afternoon of shopping. Their restaurant fare is also worth stopping by for, more health-conscious than the decadent décor might suggest.

CLUB STYLE
22 Sous les Joups
157

DOWN-TO-EARTH CAFÉ
23 Chez Camille
8, rue Ravignan, 18th

Yellow seems to be a favoured colour for funky Parisian cafés, and this calming slice of bohemia has certainly had the yellow treatment, which makes it feel all the more relaxed and welcoming. So, too, do the chess- and backgammon boards and the Scrabble games. If the games don't grab you, you can enjoy the elevated view, then walk through the lovely place Emile Goudeau, which has been home to a number of Montmartre artists over the years, including one Pablo Picasso.

HILLTOP LUXURY
24 L'Hôtel Particulier de Montmartre
118

DESIGN BY THE BOOK
25 Pages 50/70
15, rue Yvonne-le-Tac, 18th

Opposite Gaspard de la Butte (see below), the grown-up pursuit of collecting is encouraged at Olivier Verlet's Pages 50/70, which specializes in modern glass, ceramic and lighting design. There are many retro shops in Paris but Pages 50/70 continues to come top of the class (the page numbers refer to those in a book on the history of design that deal with the modern period). Alongside ceramics by Jacques Ruelland, Pol Cambost and Georges Jouve are furniture and other pieces by Pierre Guariche, Pierre Paulin and Mathieu Matégot.

CLASSY KIDS
26 Gaspard de la Butte
10 bis, rue Yvonne-le-Tac, 18th

The mohair skirts, soft flannel caps and coats and chunky graphic cardigans would be at home on the big catwalk, but in Catherine Malaure's atelier-shop it's the mouse, Gaspard, and his friends who get to show them off. Her designs for children from birth to age six are as clever and beautifully imaginative as they are well made. With a boundless supply of new ideas, sometimes resulting in as many as forty new designs in a season, Malaure claims that she never gets bored, and it's easy to see why. Here, a mere matched set of plaid trousers and hat or a textured pullover just might make you want to have children. Her designs have proved so popular that Malaure has opened another shop for grown-ups on the nearby rue d'Orsel (p. 72).

At the top of the rue des Martyrs (p. 67), the rue d'Orsel is full of delightful boutiques. Zélia sur la Terre comme au Ciel provides extravagant bridal concoctions that run from medieval princess to saucy peasant, while the Galerie Christine Diegoni fills two elegant shop spaces with furniture and objects from the 1930s to the present. Follow your nose to Senteurs de Fée and discover the origins of incense and products derived from essential oils and spices that were used in the past, but were forgotten with the advent of mechanized fragrance production. They now have a second shop on the rue de Sevigné (p. 85). In the rue des Trois Thés, Jérémie Barthod creates costume jewelry from colourful stones and finely formed metals.

Place Charles-Dullin, a peaceful and well-kept square around the pretty Théâtre de l'Atelier, offers a lovely view of the shops around and along the rue des Trois-Frères, like Mira Belle, whose hats have a frilly, flowery, far-out appeal. The theatre itself was first opened in 1822 as the Théâtre Montmartre in what was then the village of Orsel. In 1922 a young comedian, Charles Dullin, restarted the theatre and brought it acclaim between the wars. Today, it is a reliable venue for modern drama featuring work by David Leveaux, Frédéric Bélier-Garcia and Jacques Lassalle, as well as a host of international playwrights. A few doors down from the square, L'Entracte, an intimate bistro hung with taffeta draperies, offers classics done well. Scan the photos of local cabaret star and café regular, Michou.

BEAUTIFUL BOTTLES
29 Belle de Jour

7, rue Tardieu, 18th

This shop is a perfume collector's dream, filled with rare, cut-crystal pieces, from *fin-de-siècle* bottles for smelling salts to boxes for creams, hairpins and soaps, all made in the days before plastics. Pieces by Baccarat and Val St-Lambert accompany scents by Guerlain and Houbigant.

FASHION FROM BRAZIL VIA CALAIS
30 Márcia de Carvalho

2, rue des Gardes, 18th

Brazilian-born Márcia de Carvalho was one of the design pioneers on the rue des Gardes (see right), and now makes draped pieces in jersey fabric that are convertible from a wrap to a tunic, inside out and upside down. She also specializes in Calais lace, which she uses to trim pretty party dresses and bridal wear on commission.

NEW FASHION EDGE
31 Rue des Gardes

- Association Createurs Goutte d'Or, no. 6, 18th
- Luc Dognin, no. 4, 18th

This area of Montmartre, suitably close to the fabric emporium of Marché St-Pierre, has become a centre for young creatives to launch their wares. Just up from the rue de la Goutte d'Or at no. 6 is a shop with no name that features a group of designers at a time. The work of Katia Lauranti, including ethnic, voluminous kaftans in textured fabrics that have been trimmed in silk or contrasting solid and ornately patterned materials, has been shown alongside the bold bustiers and corsets of Sylviane Nuffer, designed for both men and women. Next door, at no. 4, Luc Dognin continues to turn out delightfully shaped, creamy leather bags. Despite their elegant forms, it is their beautifully painted linings and concealed pockets that have eager shoppers yanking open purses all over Paris.

CUT FROM A UNIQUE CLOTH

32 Lily Latifi

11, rue des Gardes, 18th

One of the successes of the rue des Gardes (see also p. 73) is Lily Latifi, whose shop on the corner of rue Polonceau is a showcase for her range of clothing, accessories, interiors and gift items. The young Franco-Iranian designer crosses the boundaries of applied and visual arts and industrial design to create fabrics that she forms into unique objects. Artist and craftswoman Latifi's aim is to 'develop new tactile materials for soft furnishings', which form the basis of her designs: her 'etna' collection features a vertically striped fabric used for sarongs, floor lamps and handbags. The most striking objects in the shop are the sharply cut felt bags and accessories and puzzle-piece floor coverings in felt that can be fitted together, all favouring strong reds and blues as well as beige and black.

HIGH-STYLE BRASSERIE

33 Le Soleil

109, avenue Michelet, 18th

One thing you should know before you get inside: it may look like a bistro, but it definitely isn't. Run by a former 'food hunter' who once worked for some three-star chefs and now seeks out the best products all around the country, Le Soleil is an upper-class brasserie, chic and cosy, offering quite simple food extremely well prepared (simplicity can sometimes be very luxurious). Try the green bean salad, any fresh fish (the owner loves seafood), roasted pigeon, the 350-gram *entrecôte* steak with a red wine sauce or the huge rum baba (don't even try to eat it on your own). The message at Le Soleil is that the best products often make the best cooking.

BISTRO RETRO

34 Chéri Bibi

15, rue André del Sarte, 18th

Chéri Bibi is a pretty thing of a bistro a few steps away from the *butte* of Montmartre, chock-full of vintage furniture from the 1950s and Scandinavian 1960s. The tables are tightly set together, the clientele is hip and the daily dishes are written on a chalkboard. The menu, shunning over-complexity, chooses to play the classic bistro répertoire. A flawless *pâté de tête* is sliced at your table, lentils are served directly from the bowl, thick-cut chips escort plump sausages made by the trendiest butcher in town. The lamb shoulder is served as an order for two; wines are wicked, the check is not. So what do you say? Yum!

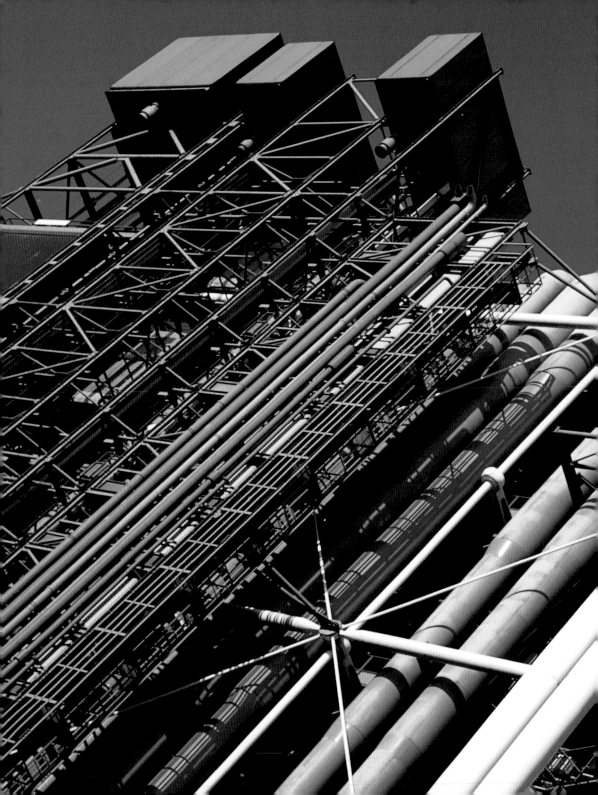

Beaubourg
Marais
Canal St-Martin

Whatever your opinion of the high-tech nakedness of the Centre Pompidou (p. 80), there is no escaping its role as an inspiration and symbol of new design, as the shops and galleries in the surrounding Beaubourg neighbourhood have demonstrated since the building's completion in the 1970s. Going east into the Marais, literally 'the swamp', the Musée Carnavalet and the elegant place des Vosges signal another era entirely, as do the many lovely 16th- and 17th-century *hôtels particuliers* that were built to house personalities almost as grand as the architecture. The Marais also has historic associations with craftspeople, a reputation that has been given a recent polish, as young Parisian and international couturiers, artisans and design specialists congregate in areas like the rue Vieille-du-Temple (p. 87) and the small but finely tuned atelier-galleries around its northern end and on the rue de Poitou (p. 90). The rue Charlot (p. 93) is increasingly popular, though still home to some of the area's most innovative designers, based in old residential or industrial buildings that have been spruced up or working in small cooperatives, whose talents are not yet matched by their turnover. On the rue du Roi-de-Sicile and rue des Rosiers you will find fashion boutiques with as much originality as the big names on the Left Bank, but with premises (and prices) that are decidedly less opulent. Throughout the creative density of the 3rd and 4th arrondissements are bookshops, exhibition spaces and bars tucked between and around the historic sites. Aided and abetted by a spirited gay population, this is also home to some of the liveliest café culture in Paris, with old favourites and trendy hotspots filling out a night-time destination for those seeking contemporary style tinged with the romance of historic architecture.

The hive of creativity has been spreading steadily northwards to the latest of Paris's rejuvenated areas, the hip, bohemian and village-like Canal St-Martin in the 10th arrondissement. Perhaps this is because lower rents have lured designers, architects and media start-ups in the area; or perhaps it's because the trains from London decant their international visitors hourly at the Gare du Nord a few blocks away. No matter — a visit to the shops and groovy cafés of the canal area, especially after spending time around the tourist hubs, is like travelling to a rural French town (especially when the quai de Valmy is closed for pedestrians) with urban sophistication. Drinking or dining canalside today is calmer, cooler, less frenetic and showy than the Left Bank or even the Marais. It's a place where the aesthetic dynamism of Paris feels accessible and personable in a way that it must have once done before the tour buses and chain stores moved in.

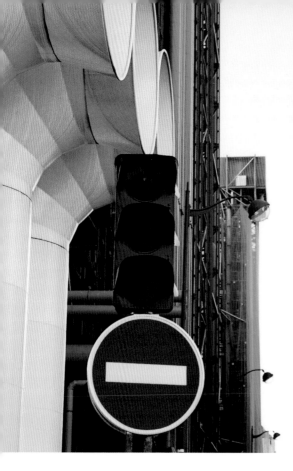

HIGH-TECH LANDMARK

1 Centre Pompidou

place Georges Pompidou, 4th

AN EVEN NEWER TWIST

2 Georges

Centre Pompidou, 6th floor, 4th

Some people find it amusing that a conservative politician such as Georges Pompidou fostered such avant-garde architectural projects as this extraordinary work by Richard Rogers and Renzo Piano. As striking as it is today, it certainly caused a few jaws to drop when it was opened in 1977, with its exposed servicing pipes and framework jutting up from the old Beaubourg neighbourhood. But the building, with its contemporary art galleries, has lived to be loved and a revamp in 2000, which included the addition of a rooftop restaurant (see Georges; right), has given it a new lease of life.

This is another piece of the Costes brothers' empire, on the sixth floor of the Pompidou and with breathtaking views over the city's rooftops, probably the best view you can get from a restaurant anywhere in the city. Most interesting is the unusual architecture, designed by Dominique Jakob and Brendan MacFarlane (see also Florence Loewy; p. 88), a strange mixture of space-age influences and hollowed-out organic shapes, alternating with icy aluminium and splashes of colour – cold and shiny on the outside, warm and inviting inside. Booking is a good idea for dinner, but you can just turn up and have a drink in one of the organic-shaped pods, or, early on, a cocktail on the roof terrace.

DUCASSE REINVENTION

3 Benoît

20, rue St-Martin, 4th

DESIGN LINES

4 FR66

25, rue du Renard, 4th

Benoît has been proudly catering to a choice clientele since 1912. Indeed, this is one of the oldest bistros in Paris. While its old-fashioned charm is one of the primary reasons for going there, the place, now fallen into the hands of Alain Ducasse (see p. 147), is worth a visit in its own right. Go there for lunch (prices are steeper at dinner time), and take a round trip to a faraway era when food meant business: meat pie, turbot in Champagne sauce, scallops *à la Grenobloise* (heavily buttered, dieters beware), gigantic cassoulet, calf's head, chocolate profiteroles. After such a feast, count on three hours of steady walking around the Beaubourg neighbourhood to make it go down.

This design furniture shop is the genuine article. Three designers – Christophe Pillet, Jean-Marie Massaud and Dominique Mathieu – make their limited-edition furniture, lighting and objects for Maryline Brustolin and her sister Corrine, who opened this gallery, designed by architect Gilles Deseudavy, in 2001. The shop is unique in Paris, Brustolin says, in that it carries high-design furnishings for every aspect of the home, from flooring and rugs to door handles, sofas, chairs and lighting. In addition to the clean-lined pieces by their in-house designers, there is work from the Dutch collective Droog, lighting by Philippe Starck, ceramics by Marcel Wanders and amazing sponge furniture by Massayo Ave.

SIMPLY CHIC

5 Blancs Manteaux

42, rue des Blancs-Manteaux, 4th

This unassuming little shop near the corner of the rue du Temple looks much like a stockroom, as designers Alain Camliset and Junji Tominaga pack shipments for their mostly long-distance clientele. But don't be put off by the boxes and the cramped space. Camliset is always happy to have walk-in customers, though you may have to ring the bell to call him from the workroom downstairs. Look for smart Audrey Hepburn-style suits in some of the most colourfully inventive tweeds and wool prints you'll see, and note the bright, contrasting linings, trim wool coats and a small selection of footwear.

THE HAMMAM TREATMENT

6 Les Bains du Marais

31–33, rue des Blancs-Manteaux, 4th

At the risk of employing a much-used term, the Marais baths really are an oasis in the city. Not just the services, of which there are many, but immediately in the entrance, where warm wood and cool tile, plants and spicy aromas greet visitors. There is a salon on the left and a bank of wood and glass cabinets full of impeccable rows of beauty and skincare products to the right. Straight ahead is a little café where clients can have a snack, drink or health-enhancing meal. In the Bains du Marais, you can have your hair cut and coloured, you can be manicured, pedicured or waxed, have a purifying facial or sauna or hammam treatment and a variety of massages with or without essential oils. The baths are open to women Monday through Wednesday, and to men Thursday through Saturday. Weekends are mixed, so clients must wear bathing suits.

SUGAR AND SPICE

7 Pain de Sucres

14, rue Rambuteau, 3rd

The young duo behind this splendid shop of sweet things worked with Michelin-starred chef Pierre Gagnaire (see p. 142), so it's no wonder that the presentations in the window make you stop and stare and maybe take a photo or two. As well as sticky concoctions of lemony cream, beautifully iced cakes topped with a perfect raspberry and coloured macaroons, expect a surprising use of herbs such as rosemary or jasmine. They've also perfected a savoury *pain spécial* that resembles a *pain au chocolat*, but is filled with things like tomato and black olives.

FEMININE FEELING

8 Azzedine Alaïa

175

FASHIONABLE RETREAT

9 3Rooms

130

GOTHIC REVIVAL REVISITED

10 Hôtel Bourg Tibourg

120

FASHIONABLE SIDE

11 Rue du Bourg-Tibourg

- 0044, no. 16, 4th
- Rautureau, no. 16, 4th
- Delphine-Charlotte Parmentier, no. 26
- Coude Fou, no. 12
- Mariage Frères, no. 35

This quiet street, home to the jewel-box Hôtel Bourg Tibourg (p. 120), is a unique mix of modern style and old Parisian charm. The most cutting-edge fashions are found at 0044, where clothing for men and women designed in Paris and made in France is both streetwise and sophisticated. A dramatic interior shows off cowhide boots, or spiky cuffs alongside cool draped styles for women and similarly androgynous designs for men; black and beige are the reigning hues. Jean-Baptiste Rautureau, whose women's shoe designs can be found in the Free Lance brand, has a similarly edgy shop with challenging footwear for men, while farther along at no. 26, Delphine-Charlotte Parmentier's dynamic and delicate jewelry pieces, *cloisonné*, leather work and lace created in the old studio she inherited from her grandparents are a world away. Parmentier started out designing accessories for Jeanne Lanvin, Thierry Mugler and Claude Montana, and recently created a jewelry collection for Swarovski. Coude Fou is a bright no-nonsense bar well off the track of the partying hordes that invade the Marais of a weekend evening. Yet more civilized refreshment can be had from one of the city's oldest tea retailers, Mariage Frères, whose rooms are like a step back toward a more genteel period.

CONTEMPORARY CLASSICS

12 Sentou Galerie

163

mon Vieil ami
a f a i m

demi-court-bouillon, ensuite les laisser égoutter sans les

13 Mon Vieil Ami
69, rue St-Louis-en-l'Île, 4th

The British would call this a 'gastropub'. The concept hasn't crossed the Channel though, so let's call it a 'modern inn'. The walls may be stone but the design, like the cooking, suggests a certain subtle refinement. The success of the place really is all about the totally relaxed mood, and simple yet sexy yet homely yet sophisticated food staged in a surrounding mix of clever design and architectural heritage. The young chef, supervised by the not-so-young, three-Michelin-starred Antoine Westermann from Strasbourg, might produce slow-cooked vegetables with onions and sardines or veal kidneys in Pinot Noir followed by *gratiné* Mirabelle plums, all to be eaten at a vast table shared by genuine Parisians and British tourists alike.

ENCHANTED ISLE
14 Île St-Louis
- Berthillon, 31, rue St-Louis-en-l'Île, 4th
- Brasserie de l'Île St-Louis, 55, quai de Bourbon, 4th
- Église St-Louis-en-Île, 19 bis, rue St-Louis-en-Île, 4th

Somewhat less visited than its sister island, the smaller Île St-Louis retains its elegant appearance with grand townhouses, designed by the fashionable builder Louis Le Vau in the early 17th century, that are still some of the most expensive real estate in Paris. The picturesque narrow cobbled streets were home at different times to Baudelaire, Racine, La Fontaine and Molière, and are now full of charming boutiques, art galleries and cafés such as the lovely Berthillon, famous for its many unique fruit sorbets (and sadly closed during most of the summer), and the old style Brasserie de l'Île St-Louis. For a more memorable meal, visit Mon Vieil Ami (see above). The Église St-Louis-en-Île, also designed by Le Vau, has a Baroque interior that you can enjoy while attending one of the classical music concerts performed inside.

BIO-COSMETIC WORKSHOP
15 Canzi
4, rue Ferdinand Duval, 4th

Canzi was created by Stéphane Mottay, who began his business in Washington, DC taking clients by appointment only. His aim is to find the best products for individual skin and hair types drawing from his own products (created out of his research into bio-cosmetics) and those he deems worthy, all of which are organic.

With a counter specially designed by architect Stéphane Perrin to convert into a 'laboratory table', Mottay offers weekly *ateliers-beauté*, or 'beauty workshops', during which he helps clients to mix their own potions using his well-chosen ingredients, including fresh plant material without preservatives (meaning it can't be stored for very long), even adding their choice of scent. All products come in distinctive packaging and an exhortation to think fresh and organic thoughts when it comes to your skin.

BURGUNDIAN CHARMS
16 Au Bourguignon du Marais
52, rue François-Miron, 4th

Would you sell your soul to the devil for a Pinot Noir or a Chardonnay? Then you'll probably be glad to learn that this fancy bistro has a cellarful of upper-class wines from Burgundy, and not necessarily expensive ones, which is quite unusual. If you're not sure what to choose, ask owner Jacques Bavard (whose name means 'talkative'); he'll be sure to unearth a secret bottle that will go well with Burgundian snails, a large slice of *jambon persillé*, *œufs en meurette* (traditional poached eggs in a red wine sauce) or *andouillette* (chitterling sausage) from the famous producer Duval. Some might even call that heaven.

ÉLÉGANCE SUPRÊME
17 L'Ambroisie

138

CULTURAL OFFSHOOTS
18 Rue de Sévigné
- Comptoir de l'Image, no. 44, 3rd
- Galerie Chez Valentin, 9, rue St-Gilles, 3rd

Madame de Sévigné, the famed 18th-century literary lady, was one of the early occupants of the newly built Marais mansions. Now the notable stops include the fashion photography bookshop Comptoir de l'Image, opened by a former assistant to Richard Avedon. The Galerie Chez Valentin was designed by Jean-Michel Wilmotte (see MK2 Bibliothèque; p. 26) for owners Philippe and Fréderique Valentin to show experimental work in video, photography and installations.

ROCOCO ART AND DECORATION

19 Le Musée Cognacq-Jay

8, rue Elzévir, 3rd

Like the extravagant Musée Jacquemart André (p. 64), the smaller and more intimate Cognacq-Jay is the result of a private collection donated by individuals to the city of Paris. Ernest Cognacq founded the Samaritaine department store in 1900, and used his increasing fortune to buy art, antiques and decorative objects that now adorn the 16th-century Hôtel Donan, which was refurbished to provide a setting for this amazing collection of largely 18th-century art and furnishings. Entire suites of furniture are arranged with complementary period *boiserie*, carpets and paintings.

OUT OF AFRIQUE

20 Rue Elzévir

- La Boutique de la CSAO, no. 9, 3rd
- Le Petit Dakar, no. 6, 3rd
- La Galerie 3A, no. 9, 3rd
- Le Jokko, no. 5, 3rd

This small street in the Marais has erupted in colourful tribute to African influences courtesy of Valérie Schlumberger, who spends her time scouring the fairs and markets of West Africa. She also founded the Compaignie du Sénegal et de l'Afrique de l'Ouest (CSAO), which became a starting point for La Boutique, selling hand-picked crafts and art. Next came the café Le Petit Dakar, serving Senegalese and African specialities, and La Galerie 3A, showing contemporary African art. In 2003, Schlumberger opened the bar, exhibition space and live music venue Le Jokko with musician Youssou N'dour.

ARCHITECTURE AND ART

21 La Galerie d'Architecture

11, rue des Blancs-Manteaux, 4th

Architects Gian Mauro Maurizio and Olga Pugliese set up their intimate modern white space in 1999 'to show the work of contemporary architects in an alternative space, to show what is going on now with architecture and to show the work of young architects as well as the more famous'. The gallery focuses on Europe, but they have also exhibited work from Japan and the US. A small café and bookshop make this a great place for a quick architecture injection.

PIÈCE UNIQUE

22 A-poc

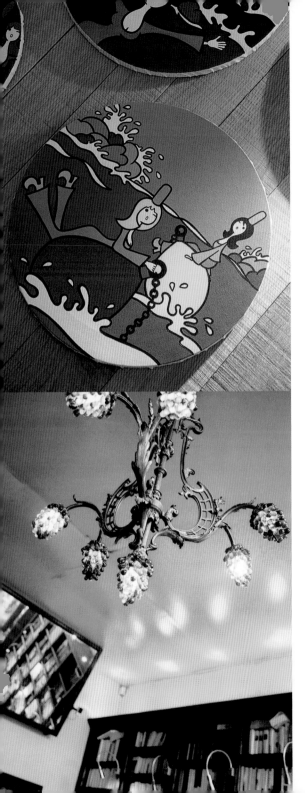

23 Rue Vieille-du-Temple

- La Belle Hortense, no. 31, 4th
- Café du Trésor, 7–9, rue du Trésor, 4th
- L'Étoile Manquante, no. 34, 4th
- ToolsGalerie, no. 119, 3rd

The recent upsurge of galleries, boutiques, bars and restaurants only adds to this street's medieval charm. Among the noisier and more exuberant gay bars, La Belle Hortense sets a quieter tone, with bottles of Côtes du Rhône and Châteauneuf du Pape sharing window space with books by Paul Celan and Martin Broda, whereas on the strangely quiet and pedestrianized rue du Trésor, the Café du Trésor boasts an array of rooms decorated in a sort of futuristic Baroque. L'Étoile Manquante is one of the better popular bar-restaurants in this area. A good place for a relaxing drink, a cocktail or a bite to eat (note the train running through the restroom). Fashion designers have colonized the street farther north of the cafés and bars. Jamin Puech (p. 171) and Martin Grant (p. 88) have moved into the area, and Tatiana Lebedev (see FuturWare Lab, p. 69) has her second shop here at no. 64. ToolsGalerie has been attracting the attention of modern collectors since 2003 with its focus on French and European contemporary designers, such as Maarten Baas, Richard Hutten, Frederic Ruyant and Marcel Wanders

ARTISAN-MADE BAGS AND SHOES

24 Jamin-Puech

171

GREAT GALETTES

25 Breizh Café

109, rue Vieille-du-Temple, 3rd

One would think a Breton buckwheat pancake should be simple, but a good *galette* is hard to find. All the more reason to check out the Breizh Café's third location (after Cancale, Brittany, and even Tokyo) and make sure they got it right. In the pop-inspired décor, you may (re)discover the sheer happiness of a buckwheat *galette* with smoked butter by Jean-Yves Bordier, before surrendering to a plate of country chitterling sausage or utterly delicious Tsarkaya oysters, with a whole battalion of excellent organic ciders or a cool Lancelot beer on hand to help them go down. The best place for a snack after raiding the fashion stores in the upper Marais.

26 Archibooks
18–20, rue de la Perle, 3rd

Much more than a minimally designed architecture bookshop, Archibooks is the headquarters for a specialized imprint started by Christophe le Gac, editor-in-chief and publisher of the architecture magazine *Archistorm*, and Marc Sautereau, head of the Bookstorming bookshops. Their aim is to publish five books each year on art, architecture and design between their signature thick-cut plain cardboard covers. The first of their series was a monograph of the artist Bernard Calet. *Archistorm* books are on sale alongside the shop's generous selection of international art, architecture and design titles.

FRENCH ARTS AND CRAFTS
27 Collection
4, rue de Thorigny, 3rd

The Ateliers d'Art de France (French Federation for Craft Professionals) has opened a permanent exhibition space and gallery that showcases works of decorative art and craft by French makers. The airy modern interior is a new venue for the organization, which was founded in 1868 and helps bring the work of individual craft workers and artists to the public. Expect to find unique pieces by young artists as well as exhibitions year-round. Collection and its boutiques located in the 17th also do work to commission.

THE ART OF BOOKS
28 Florence Loewy
9–11, rue de Thorigny, 3rd

Where better to demonstrate the beauty and utility of architecture than in an architecture and art bookshop? At Florence Loewy, architects Dominique Jakob and Brendan MacFarlane, whose modular interventions are in evidence at the Georges restaurant (p. 80), took an architects' favoured material, birch-ply, and created curving compartmental towers to accommodate the wide range of books in a relatively small Parisian shop space. Look carefully and you can see the books stored ingeniously behind the other titles. The stock itself is a wide range of volumes in many languages on contemporary art, architecture, design and graphics. There is also a small exhibition space.

PARLOUR GAMES
29 L'Apparemment Café
18, rue des Coutures-St-Gervais, 3rd

In Paris there are cafés that combine wine and car culture, wine and film, wine and gourmet delicacies, and here we have wine and games ('apparently', hence the name). In these cosy, wood-panelled rooms just opposite the Musée Picasso and among the many arty boutiques and galleries of the Marais, you can take a culture break of sorts, order a glass or bottle and settle into a leather armchair for a quick game of cards or challenge someone to one of several board games. Otherwise, it's a good place to stop and mull over your purchases from the neighbouring bookshops (see Archibooks and Florence Loewy; left).

HIDDEN TREASURES
30 Les Archives de la Presse
51, rue des Archives, 3rd

If you are one of those people who gets a shiver down the spine reading a copy of *Vogue* from the 1960s, then the Archives de la Presse just might be your idea of heaven. A treasure trove for art directors and fashionistas looking for ideas, the store specializes in vintage publications of sports, fashion, cinema, travel and cookery, as well as storing miles of old newspapers. There are hundreds of back issues of *Vogue*, *Marie Claire* and *Paris Match*, including a special collection dedicated to magazines featuring Diana, Princess of Wales since her first press appearance. The staff are indispensable and, as they say, 'very organized'.

TAILOR TRIM
31 Martin Grant
10, rue Charlot, 3rd

Australian designer Martin Grant has relocated, but keeps the Marais as home to his carefully crafted pieces that sing out with style. Grant has a penchant for darts, high up all along the waist and even at the elbows. His needlecord jackets, all with matching trousers, feature narrow, accordion-style pleats running vertically further to tailor the heavy fabric to the body. Similarly his 'Priest Coat', in angora, wool or calfskin, is tightened up with darted waist and arms. It all makes for a smart, crisp, very tailored look. Blouses are lighter-weight and brighter, but the four-button cuff and substantial collar mean that 'blousy' is somebody else's idea of fashion.

DISCOUNT DESIGNER WEAR
32 L'Habilleur
44, rue de Poitou, 3rd

If you've always thought that the latest prêt-à-porter designs were beyond your bank account, then you'll be pleased to happen upon this small bounty of a discount shop. The selection is dominated by womenswear, but there are also men's clothes from such big names as Paul et Joe, John Richmond, Plein Sud, Vivienne Westwood and Patrick Cox at around half-price. The collections follow the same fashion-season cycle but one year later, so these are all ever so slightly dated but no less striking.

VINTAGE AND NEW
33 Rue de Poitou
• Galerie de l'Instant, no. 46, 3rd
• Muskhane, 3, rue Pastourelle, 3rd
• The Collection, no. 33, 3rd

New designers seem to be popping up on the rue de Poitou at a rather startling rate, perhaps encouraged by the arrival of the Christian Lacroix-designed Hôtel du Petit Moulin around the corner. Julia Gragnon opened her small gallery at no. 46 to present the work of her father François Gragnon, as well as style-setting vintage photographs by Olivier Dassault and others. At Muskhane, Thierry and Valerie Billot have sourced all of their fabric in Nepal to make an array of colourful products for the home in felt, cashmere and chambray, from whimsical bunny slippers to tasteful cushions, bags and scarves. At no. 33, The Collection offers fresh designs in wallcoverings, furnishings and lighting by French and international designers.

CUTTING-EDGE CREATIONS
34 Rue des Filles du Calvaire
• Lieu Commun, no. 5, 3rd
• Les Lunetiers Delambre, no.10, 3rd
• Balouga, no. 25, 3rd

This little street has begun attracting its own share of creative types. At Lieu Commun, you'll find quirky and inspiring items such as graphic T-shirts and surreal vessels by Matali Crasset, Blonde Music and Misericordia, while across the way, alternative optician Christian Gluckman with creative partner Fabien Sovant offers more than a pair of glasses; the cutting-edge eyewear, including Gluckman's own designs, set against an avant-garde backdrop lined in blond wood, are about making a style statement. Meanwhile, Balouga has latched on to the trend for high-design and high-quality furniture and objects for kids.

35 Rue Charlot

- Passage de Retz, no. 9, 3rd
- Moon Young Hee, no. 62, 3rd

The formerly disused spaces on the rue Charlot have become magnets for creatives and creative reuse. At Passage de Retz, this former toy factory in the Marais has been turned into a clean and bright contemporary gallery that hosts local artistic happenings. Entering through the large wood doors into a quiet courtyard, you head right into the small museum shop selling funky items and books. Next to the bookshop is a 1950s-inspired café created by designer Christian Biecher. It's a quiet and groovy place for coffee and snacks. Continuing on, the atelier and shop of Korean designer Moon Young Hee is set in a space of unfinished stone walls, where patterns and scraps line the floor and her delicate, diaphanous garments hang beautifully but rather unceremoniously on modest rails.

NATURE'S GRAPHICS

36 Dominique Picquier

170

CRAZY, SEXY, COOL

37 Murano Urban Resort

124

FAR OUT, BABY

38 Murano Urban Resort Bar

158

FUGITIVE OENOPHILIA

39 Le Verre Volé

152

TEA, DINNER, DRINKS

40 Rue de Lancry

- Et dans mon coeur il y a, no. 56, 10th
- Couleurs Canal, no. 56, 10th
- Le Cinquante, no. 50, 10th

Just off the canalside quai de Valmy, the rue de Lancry is bursting with inspired little spots for eating and drinking. You'll be struck by the warm red wine-coloured and candlelit interior of corner restaurant Et dans mon coeur il y a. Chef Benoît Mathurin, previously of Lasserre and L'Aubergine, produces a menu that is creative but sound in an atmosphere that's friendly and well served. If you're not yet ready for a full meal, try Couleurs Canal (a bit farther up the road but sharing the same street number),

a funky little tea salon full of interesting blends and sweet snacks. Later in the evening, the formica tables at the 1950s-style bar Le Cinquante start to fill up. Cocktails are a bit more up-to-date than the name suggests, as is the atmosphere, populated with the new trendies of the 10th.

CANALSIDE CAFÉ

41 La Marine

55 bis, quai de Valmy, 10th

It's often packed, with its bright-red frontage framing reassuringly worn interiors and its prime site along the canal making it immediately attractive even to those who have never been inside. The creative, youthful atmosphere of the neighbourhood is also apparent, and La Marine is one of those places that survives on doing the basics well (good, unpretentious dishes and reasonable drink), and letting the spirit of the crowd do the rest. In an area that is fast becoming a favourite with hip Parisians, it won't be long before places like this are all too rare.

CAFÉ COOL

42 Chez Prune

71, quai de Valmy, 10th

On a picturesque corner of the quai de Valmy sits a funky café-bar overlooking the Canal St-Martin. The bold mustard-yellow walls, mosaic-covered tables and buzzy locals tell you that Chez Prune is not about staid café offerings. The staff are welcoming and relaxed, despite the fact that Prune has proved increasingly popular as the area attracts an ever-growing set of admirers. A worthy stop for lunch, evening tapas or drinks until 2 am, it's a favourite among media professionals and the young and fashionable. The classic menu offers a range from blood sausages to *assiettes 'faites maison'*, and the wine list is extensive, but they will just as gladly pour you a cool *pression*.

ALL THINGS BRIGHT AND BEAUTIFUL

43 Antoine et Lili

95, quai de Valmy, 10th

Antoine et Lili's 'village' is a departure from their chain of shops in and around Paris and abroad with its collection of fashion, homeware, accessories and café in separate, candy-coloured shops. 'Bright' does not begin to describe the combinations of red, orange, yellow and turquoise that serve as the backdrop to the vibrant patterns of pottery and linens that fill the Art Déco shop, along with flower-decked umbrellas, beaded belts, paisley blouses and flared trousers. Refuel in style in the fuchsia 'tea house'.

ARTY READ

44 Artazart

83, quai de Valmy, 10th

Behind the graphic orange shopfront lies not just an art bookstore, but a centre for creative endeavour. Anything between two covers that is to do with art, architecture or graphic design can be found here, as well as a host of things you wouldn't expect from a bookstore. Stop in here on a stroll along the canal to browse the latest books and magazines in several languages, but also to visit a photographic exhibition.

PRETTY IN PINK

45 Stella Cadente

93, quai de Valmy, 10th

The mauve, pink and lilac hues give the subtle signal that this is a place focused on feminine flair. The fashion label set up by designer Stanislassia Klein has quickly become a must for savvy Parisian women and for those who just like the soft, unusual details she adds to simple, pretty designs. The former tool warehouse has been given a light, romantic lift. You'll want to touch everything, from the feather-trimmed chiffon shift dresses to the beaded bags and diaphanous shawls. And this is low-pressure selling, since you won't need much convincing as you sit in a pastel sofa draped in alluring fabrics and sip a hospitable cup of tea, while considering your purchases and gazing out over the tree-shaded bridge.

IT'S ALL IN THE ATMOSPHERE

46 L'Atmosphère

49, rue Lucien-Sampaix, 10th

Just up the road from the villagey shop row of Stella Cadente (see above) and Antoine et Lili (p. 93), this is a favourite spot on the Canal St-Martin scene, with its funky mix of fresh flowers and plants, dried bunches, old furnishings and bright crockery for those reasonably priced *pichets* of wine. Outdoor seating is on the canalside and couldn't be more atmospheric. It no longer has live music at night, but does on a Sunday afternoon.

1930S CLASSIC

47 L'Hôtel du Nord

102, quai de Jemmapes, 10th

This long-awaited restoration project finally puts the old Canal St-Martin landmark firmly on the map for tourists and neighbours alike. Built in 1885, the hotel was made

famous by the eponymous 1938 film by Marcel Carné . The building later suffered a period of decline until the 1990s, when it was first renovated for public use. The current group took possession in 2005, and has accomplished another much bolder and more comprehensive renovation project which has turned the cinema-myth, former flea-bag and sometime brothel into a trendy bar and restaurant, complete with terrace, library area and *petit salon* with WiFi connection. You can even come in for afternoon tea and a game of backgammon, or just sit back and savour the mix of vintage movie paraphernalia and trendy décor with zinc bar and velvet curtains, styled on 'Paris in the '30s'.

BRETON FAVOURITES

48 Chez Michel

10, rue de Belzunce, 10th

Away from the canal area, behind a little church, there's a place where the atmosphere is more provincial than fashionably Parisian, and the décor has definitely not been the work of Philippe Starck. The main draw here is the food, cooked by chef Thierry Breton. True to his name, Breton was trained to the art of reinventing classics dug up from his native Brittany. Unsurprisingly, the fish comes out a big winner – the *brandade* (a dish of puréed cod) is made with home-salted fresh fish. Meat lovers, though, may be equally satisfied, especially during the game season when grouse, among other delicacies, is served. The wine list is beautiful and, yes, the service could be a little friendlier occasionally, but there's no way it's going to spoil the fun.

ARCHITECTURE CAFÉ

49 Café A

148, rue du Faubourg St-Martin, 10th

Part of the Maison d'Architecture, set in the cloisters of an old convent, Café A consists of a small bar and tables set out in the pretty walled garden. On the other side of the walls is a noisy traffic intersection, but inside the secluded space all is quiet and lush with greenery. Definitely worth a stop for lunch, coffee, tea or a drink in the afternoon.

THE HIPPEST HAPPENINGS

50 De la Ville Café

 159

Bercy
Bastille
Ménilmontant
Belleville

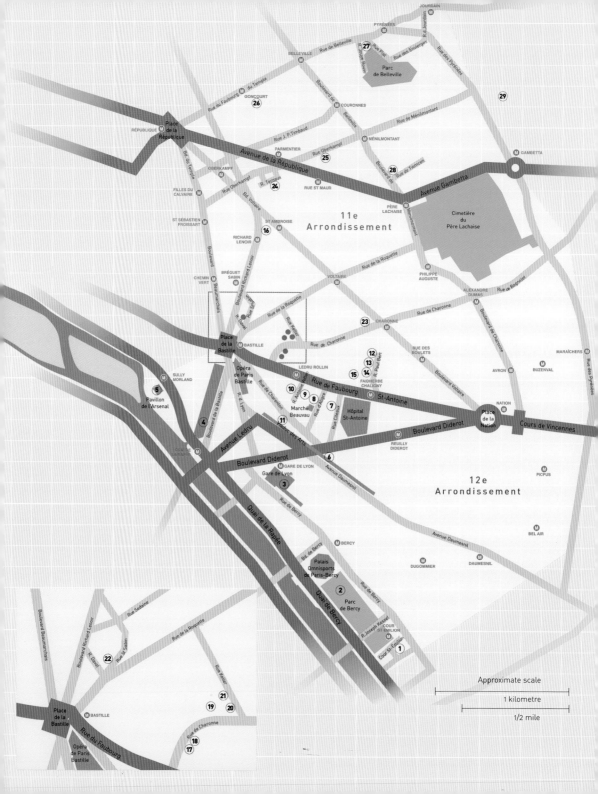

Since the French mastered the formal garden, there arose the question of what they would do for an encore. But evidence of their unbounded botanical inventiveness lies in the modern parks around the capital, such as the Parc André Citroën (p. 39) and the thoughtful mix of geometric and romantic arrangements of the vast Parc de Bercy (p. 100). While many urban capitals are bemoaning the loss of their city parks, the Parisians have developed the largest green space since Baron Haussmann boulevardized the city in the 19th century, which – together with the renovation of the former wine warehouses of the Bercy district, the construction of the large Palais Omnisports and a dedicated Métro line – has quite literally brought a breath of fresh air to an area dominated by train lines and large, inhospitable streets. It also makes a soothing introduction to the neighbourhoods to the north, which embrace urbanism in all its gritty reality.

Moving north, we encounter the avenue Daumesnil, dominated by a disused viaduct that, in a typically positive turn of regeneration, has become the home of the Viaduc des Arts (p. 103), a long varied parade of brick-arched spaces that have been restored and converted for use as modern-looking galleries and craft studios. Farther north, the Bastille beckons, with funky bars and own-design boutiques grouped around the rue de Charonne, rue Keller (p. 106) and the tiny rue Daval. In the early 1990s, the Bastille felt the flurry of regeneration, but this wasn't about new members of the *bourgeoisie* buying up old neglected warehouses and renovating them so much as club promoters looking for cheap, cavernous spaces to light up and fill with techno beats and crowds of enthusiastic dance divas. The wide, imposing avenues radiating from the place de la Bastille and the place de la République were never going to have the sparkle of the Champs-Élysées, but they were going to have an ample supply of street cred, which hasn't been entirely lost despite the neighbourhood's popularity with younger tourists. Restaurants and cafés range from the old workers' haunts to the new and enterprising, with some of the more stylish establishments setting up east in the neighbourhood of the rue de Faubourg-St-Antoine and the rue Paul-Bert.

The place de la République and the rue Oberkampf also sizzled with youthful zeal and edgy street style in the most recent Bastille revolution. They continue to buzz with café- and nightlife. Shops and bars, too, reflect the appeal of the streetwise Paris urban scene that is well away from the tourist mainstream and the heavily commercialized districts: young designers line the rue Oberkampf and appealing bars and cafés stretch even farther from the popular fray into the arty *bonhomie* of Ménilmontant and Belleville.

1 Bercy Village

- Résonances, 9-11, cour St-Émilion, 12th
- Chai 33, 33, cour St-Émilion, 12th

The actual wine stores of Bercy have also had a facelift, along with the warehouse district as a whole. The cour St-Émilion, at its heart, has its own Métro stop just after the Parc de Bercy (see below), and is now an upscale shopping parade along a cobblestoned lane. There are cafés and restaurants, where you can have tea or coffee outside or in a high-tech-rustic interior, and arty boutiques have filled the smart-looking street. Among them is the original branch of Résonances, an upmarket do-it-yourself and home speciality shop created by François Lemarchand, founder of the extremely popular Nature et Découvertes chain and responsible for Pier Import in Paris. The emphasis is on traditional, high-quality goods, such as hardware and kitchen appliances, with a modern eye for gourmet and designer products. For an altogether different experience, Thierry Bégué, the man behind Buddha Bar and Barrio Latino, created Chai 33, a huge former storehouse divided into different spaces on three levels – a wine shop, bar, lounge, restaurant and bistro, not to mention a double terrace.

GREEN GEOMETRIES

2 Parc de Bercy
quai de Bercy, 12th

It's only a few stops from the centre of town on the Métro, but it's a world away in terms of atmosphere. The Parc de Bercy was completed in 1997, the result of the redevelopment of an area dominated by old wine warehouses, a depot for the produce that was shipped to Paris by river. The development was the largest park created since the reorganization by Haussmann in the 19th century. It included the construction of the large, turf-covered Palais Omnisports de Paris-Bercy overlooking the modern landscaped Jardin de la Mémoire, which is actually a number of different green spaces that incorporate old rail lines and stone paths, as well as the existing centuries-old trees. In the tradition of formal French garden design made modern (see also Parc André Citroën; p. 39), there are geometric arrangements incorporating canals, bridges, ponds and plantings of mature trees, flowers and shrubs into a delightful space for walking, picnicking or playing. And it can now be reached from the 13th arrondissement across the Seine by way of the new footbridge (see Passerelle Simone de Beauvoir; p. 26).

NEXT STOP, BELLE ÉPOQUE
3 Le Train Bleu
Gare de Lyon, place Louis Armand, 12th

It's hard to believe, but this gorgeous Belle Époque interior with its gilt mirrors, wall paintings and medallions was for many years a rather mediocre café with a nice design. Created for the 1900 Exhibition and named after the line that used to connect Paris with Lyon and Marseille, the restaurant is a listed monument and now the cuisine has been uplifted by chef André Signoret to match the heights of decorative fancy. A red carpet runs through an enfilade of Baroque Revival rooms, where booths in carved wood sit against painted woodwork, mythical figures peer down from grand arches, and chandeliers blaze while diners enjoy classic French dishes and those at the bar sink into the leather Chesterfield sofas and feast on the spectacle.

RED ART HOUSE
4 La Maison Rouge, Fondation Antoine de Galbert
10, boulevard de la Bastille, 12th

In this formerly industrial area near the quai de la Rapée, an old factory building has been given a cutting-edge redesign by Jean-Yves Clément and now houses 2,500 square metres of exhibition space. The interior design was inspired by the idea of architectural skin, so mouldings, lighting and other surface details are highlighted. Inside the glazed façade of the existing building, a vertical red block surrounded by steel framework houses four themed exhibition rooms. There is also a bookshop and café. Check opening hours.

MODEL DEVELOPMENT
5 Pavillon de l'Arsenal
21, boulevard Morland, 4th

The Pavillon de l'Arsenal chronicles the architectural and urban history of Paris. Large-scale photographs of buildings past and present fill the walls, while scale models of the city, one of 40 square metres, afford a bird's-eye view. A recent addition by Christian Biecher is the video lounge, where red neon draws you towards a corner of individual curved polycarbonate enclosures, in which you can choose from 120 films on the work of different architects in the city and listen on your own headphones. The group video lounge is next door, where a bank of screens play a film about the city. Ongoing temporary exhibitions staged by the current big names in architecture are dynamic and informative. And it's free.

CREATIVE CAVERNS
6 Viaduc des Arts
1–129, avenue Daumesnil, 12th
- Créations Chérif, no. 13
- Maison Fey, no. 15
- Malhia, no. 19
- VIA, nos 29–35
- Le Viaduc Café, no. 43
- Vertical, no. 63
- Marie Lavande, no. 83
- Roger Lanne, no. 103

The arches of a disused railway viaduct have been cleaned up and glassed in, and now house a parade of craft shops and ateliers. Tapestries, furnishings and lighting are prominent as are gallery spaces and showrooms. Good stops include Créations Chérif, which features curvy purple, orange and red velvet sofas and chairs, and Maison Fey, which does leather-covered, stamped and embossed books, frames and furnishings. Malhia overflows with gorgeous fabrics woven on-site and in full view and available as sweaters, scarves, coats and shawls. Buy one of their reasonably priced pieces and come away with a hand-decorated Malhia bag. VIA (Valorisation de l'Innovation dans l'Ameublement), which promotes communication between designers and manufacturers, has offices and a permanent exhibition of furniture, textiles and home accessories. Le Viaduc Café has lots of pavement tables and jazz brunches on Sundays. Vertical features sculptural wood and vegetation, while Marie Lavande specializes in the conservation of fine linens using soap flakes, lavender oil and rice starch. You can watch the white-coated women, who are experts in the 17th-century technique of 'breaking and folding', hand-stitching and ironing. Buy a hand-made violin or cello from craftsman Roger Lanne, whose motto is 'work for Mozart'.

WORKERS' CHIC

7 L'Ebauchoir
43–45, rue de Cîteaux, 12th

There was a time when Paris had hundreds of places like this, mostly dedicated to a working-class clientele. Things have changed, but one can still sense that special atmosphere in this highly arty joint in the upper Bastille, where the hip and the hard-working get along pretty well. Try the place at lunchtime and you'll see what the neighbourhood must have been like fifty years ago. Leeks vinaigrette, marinated herrings with potatoes, veal liver in honey sauce, and the monumental hard-boiled egg with mayonnaise will be part of your trip back in time.

SECOND-HAND FINDS

8 Le Marché d'Aligre
place d'Aligre, 12th

If the Viaduc des Arts (p. 103) leaves you wishing for something a little more rough and ready, then a short walk around behind the viaduct will be worth your while. A small collection of traders has been gathering in the place d'Aligre since it was donated by nuns from the abbey of St-Antoine before the French Revolution. This is one of those places rumoured to be on the list of more serious dealers looking for a real 'find'. Make time for a stop at everyone's favourite African bread and pastry shop, La Ruche à Miel, on the nearby rue d'Aligre at no. 19.

THE SWEDISH CHEF

9 La Gazzetta

139

DIET BUSTERS

10 Le Square Trousseau
1, rue Antoine-Vollon, 12th

Since some fashionable designers have invaded the Bastille neighbourhood, this sublime Belle Époque bistro has become a high-profile celeb spot, where supermodels have been spotted ditching their diets for some home-made foie gras. Other nice choices are the baby chicken roasted with mustard (less than 900 calories), the steak tartare (almost fat-free), the crispy *boudin* (black pudding) with apple and cinnamon, or the black-cherry soup. The staff are cheerful and the wine list is definitely worth the trip.

LEATHER LOVES

11 Serge Amoruso
13, rue Abel, 12th

If you are someone who truly appreciates *haute maroquinerie*, then you should stop by Serge Amoruso, not just to see the fine leather goods, but also to watch the craftsmen at work in the shop. Amoruso calls himself a 'tanner and saddler, but above all a creative designer', a combination that gives his products the quality of the artisan rather than just the trend-setter (although he is also the latter). Check out the vanity case on brushed steel legs, or the postbox-style cigar pot.

SHELLFISH ON SHOW

12 L'Ecailler du Bistrot
22, rue Paul-Bert, 11th

For oyster fans visiting Paris, don't even think of going anywhere but here, one of the best fish and oyster bistros in town. During the season (the French have a saying: 'never eat oysters during the months without an "r" in the name', that is, from May to August), you'll find a dozen species, from the classic *fine de claire* to the less well-known 'Utah Beach' from Normandy. With some great bread and butter and a glass of Muscadet or Quincy, you can almost taste the sea spray.

WINE AND FOIE GRAS

13 Bistrot Paul Bert
18, rue Paul-Bert, 11th

At this appetizing and affordable bistro, the impressive owner (both for his range of wines and his knowledge) will more likely than not wish to regale you with stories about an unknown winegrower he has just met. The chef understands that his dishes must get along with the wines, and produces a cuisine that rejoices in the classic (lentil soup with foie gras, *cassoulet* with smoked Breton *andouille*). The décor is also superb, and creates a consciously old-fashioned atmosphere.

GOURMET STREET

14 Le Temps au Temps
13, rue Paul-Bert, 11th

The best bet in the area for a good meal with excellent wine in a great atmosphere is to head towards the rue Paul-Bert. Here, over no more than a hundred metres, you'll find at least three little gems, amongst which Le Temps au Temps is the most recent. The place only seats about twenty people, but is endowed with a young chef who does all the cooking by himself, in a consistently good, contemporary style. In a street where you'll be spoiled for choice, here's another one to tempt you.

15 Le Vieux Chêne
7, rue Dahomey, 11th

The French have a phrase to describe those ageing men who strive to stay young. They say, *c'est un vieux beau*, or 'an old handsome'. The Vieux Chêne ('old oak'), recently refurbished to glorious bistro beauty, could qualify for this description. Located next to the trendy rue Paul-Bert and not very far from the Bastille, it is popular with aficionados of the 1930s and antiques lovers. The oh-so-sweet owners are good at setting the right vibe to suit the place. As for the cooking, it goes well beyond the basic steak and fries, boasting fine charcuterie as well as more elaborate dishes, such as a fried 'cigar' of lobster wrapped in filo pastry, or pigeon with pak choi. The wine list is small, but perfectly formed.

16 Le Réfectoire
80, boulevard Richard Lenoir, 11th

After the success of their La Famille in the 18th, Patrick and Yannig Samot opened this Pop-Arty, school lunchroom-themed café along the rather unlovely boulevard that strikes up through the 11th. Le Réfectoire makes its own bright spot with trendy interiors featuring giant Jax lamps, chalkboard walls, complete with grammar exercises, and a pretty wild floor in the loo. Food is much better than the small size and funky arthouse touches would suggest: starters of asparagus with perfectly boiled egg or creamy leek soup, main courses of veal with fennel and polenta, and tuna encrusted with Thai basil. Lunches are usually a set menu, at last visit Fridays served up fantastic *moules et frites* – and all for (almost) school-dinner money.

17 Le Café du Passage
12, rue de Charonne, 11th

Paris should have dozens of bars like this one, especially for true wine lovers who like a laid-back atmosphere. Situated near the Bastille, Le Café du Passage offers more than 300 different wines, most of them from the so-called 'new vineyards' (from the Languedoc-Roussillon and the Rhône and Loire valleys), boasting great vintages and reasonably priced. Food is not forgotten: nice plates of fine charcuteries, a classic but perfectly tasty steak tartare, or some well-cooked pasta.

18 Isabel Marant
172

19 Galerie Patrick Seguin
5, rue des Taillandiers, 11th

Specializing in French furniture and objects from the 1950s, the gallery carries pieces by Le Corbusier, Alexandre Noll, Georges Jouve, Jean Royère, Charlotte Perriand and Serge Mouille, and there is a particular focus on Jean Prouvé. The large showroom on the rue des Taillandiers had a design overhaul by Jean Nouvel in 2003. Seguin also hosts regular exhibitions.

20 Rue Keller
• Le Souk, no. 1, 11th
• Gaëlle Barré, no. 17, 11th

This street of regeneration has resulted in some highly creative tenants: galleries, design shops, bars and ethnic restaurants. Past the open pots of spices and queues of hopeful diners at Le Souk, one of the most atmospheric North African joints in Paris, you carry the scent to the tactile joy of Gaëlle Barré, full of soft mohair creations and monochrome printed fabrics. Barré personally looks for the kind of goat that will produce her favoured material, which she turns into suits with printed trims and shift dresses that come in a variety of textures, all demonstrating her flair for invention. The street is also home to a number of boutiques selling vintage and clubwear.

21 Anne Willi
13, rue Keller, 11th

This atelier and shop has the look of a sumptuous treasure trove, for Anne Willi searches the globe for the most beautiful, luxurious fabrics, some of which might be piled on the floor when you stop by. After spending some time in Tel Aviv, where she opened a boutique, Willi returned to Paris in 1998 and was an early entrepreneur on the rue Keller. Fabric in hand, she creates elegant, long tunic-style frocks, trousers, dresses and pieces that can work as two different functions. Worsted wool, felt, crêpe, flannel and synthetics in deep solid colours or tulle woven with light, gauzy details are just some of the fabrics she uses to create her elegant pieces, some of which are reversible with contrasting colours.

Soupe du Jour
Artichauts Mozzarella à l'Italienne
Filets de Hareng Extra Doux
6 Escargots de Bourgogne
Carpaccio d'Aubergines
Antipasti
Melon au Jambon de Paris
Saumon du Chef
Filet de Rouget à la Provençale
Pavé de Veau Persillé
Noisettes d'Agneau Grillées
Entrecôte Grillée, Gratin
Pavé de Rumsteak au Poivre
Suprême au Chocolat Noir
Crème Brûlée
Salade de Fruits Exotiques
Tartes Maison
Fraises au Sucre
Figues au Vin Rouge

A DRINK AND A CHAT
22 Café de l'Industrie
16, rue St-Sabin, 11th

Among the confluence of cool urban bars and cafés around the Bastille, this is one of the better ones in terms of décor and one of the friendliest (though maybe not the most efficient) in terms of service. It's casual, with lots of potted plants, usually crowded but with a cheerful atmosphere, as it's not part of the usual tourist procession of drinking spots. Light meals are served, but most visitors just come for a drink and a chat, or to linger in the warm red booths. Now there is a second version on the opposite side of the street. So take your pick.

NEW WINES AND FOOD
23 La Muse Vin
101, rue de Charonne, 11th

Wine shops used to sell wine. Today, more often than not, they also strive to serve food. The two young owners here run a funky bistro in which to show off the best of today's winemaking. So why not stop by, sit back and enjoy under their expert guidance a selection of Chitry, St-Joseph, St-Chinian, or something delightful from the Loire valley? On the kitchen front, modern classics of roasted vegetables or red pesto swordfish make tasty accompaniments. The only drawback to the whole experience is for those who will mind the surrounding cloud of cigarette smoke.

NEIGHBOURHOOD STAR
24 Le Villaret

142

BOHEMIAN COUTURE
25 Onze
11, rue Oberkampf, 11th

A former stylist for large couture houses, Chantal Fortin brings together the work of international designers with 'complementary inspiration'. This means a very select range of womenswear, shoes and accessories that suit a particularly boho-chic taste. In this neighbourhood of changing fortunes, her boutiques have stood the test of time, drawing clientele from all around Paris to her pretty shop, with its floral rugs, vintage velvet furniture and beaded lampshades, where she offers a range of independent French and European designers, who all offer high-quality fabrics and beautiful detailing that looks hand-made even if it isn't.

BISTRO-CHIC IN BELLEVILLE
26 Le Chateaubriand

145

ARGENTINIAN JIVE
27 Le Baratin

153

RETRO-FUTURE BAR
28 La Mère Lachaise
78, boulevard de Ménilmontant, 20th

La Mère Lachaise is not one of the latest generation of trendy, high-design bars, but it does offer a variety of charms. First and foremost is the fabulous terrace on the boulevard de Ménilmontant, and second is its combination of the trendy artiness of the neighbourhood, together with a casual ease. Inside, the two rooms are decorated in complementary but distinctly different themes: old and new. One room is a sort of retro hall, the other has silver upholstered walls hung with portraits by Araki. It's often crowded and boasts a fan base of celebrities and locals.

THE GOOD OLD DAYS
29 Chez les 'On'
49, rue de la Chine, 20th

Well off the beaten track, this thoroughly Parisian bistro might have been frozen in the mid-1950s; the unchanged style of borderline kitsch and the seemingly out-of-date cooking make for a totally picturesque impression. Then again, there's nothing like a good *andouillette* accompanied by top-notch *frites* to pick you up after a long morning stroll across the Père Lachaise. Especially when washed down with a genuine Burgundy or a powerful Minervois selected from the short but faultless wine list.

Style Traveller

sleep

Paris may still be a city of grand hotels, but recent years have seen a breath of modernity enter the realm of once chintzy and gilded establishments. If you know where to look – and what you're looking for – Paris offers a complete spectrum of guest experiences behind its noble façades – from Empire chic to lush exotica. Boutique hotels with charisma are dotted through the metropolis, and a handful of illustrious establishments have been given contemporary makeovers. The hotels below represent a select guide catering to the most refined, demanding and idiosyncratic tastes.

LAVISH LACROIX

30 **Le Bellechasse**

14 8, rue de Bellechasse, 7th

Rooms from €290

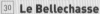

Christian Lacroix first made his mark on the Paris boutique-hotel scene with the Petit Moulin in the northern reaches of the Marais. This is his second venture, opened in 2007, and the designer has lost none of his exuberance. It's all a riot of decorative fantasy that Lacroix hopes will impart the sense of *le voyage dans le voyage* and reflect, in this area of grand old mansions, a very Parisian mix of traditional and avant-garde. Though the lobby is notable for some bold colours and a plush purple velvet sofa here and there, it is the rooms that are a visual feast. Or rather, they are a carnival of patterns, textures and themes, which draws some attention away from the fact that many are quite compact, though this doesn't seem to matter when you are surrounded by such decorative riches.

The thirty-four rooms are arranged across two buildings, all decorated according to seven themes that include the 'Tuileries', 'Patchwork', the 'Avengers' (in homage to the 1960s British television show), and the 'Mosquetaires', inspired by 17th-century paintings but with a bold, contemporary Lacroix twist. Wallcoverings were specially designed for each theme and extend across ceilings, bursting with the signature butterflies, Victorian figures imposed on a multi-coloured background, astrological motifs, or medieval characters in cartoon vibrancy parading behind the flat-screen TV. Then there are the fabrics (velvet, silk, devoré, or all three), the crocodile-textured walls, the free-standing bath sat open plan-style opposite the bed (or secreted away behind tinted glass). Two lower-ground patio rooms have tiled floors and a more minimal environment, though not a spot has missed the Lacroix magic: even the lifts have been adorned and perfumed. A 'French-style' breakfast (fresh fruit, pastries, juices, eggs) is served in the basement, a sort of rustic baroque space with stone walls and candelabra. Though it isn't visually calming, the hotel is well soundproofed so that even so close to the Musée d'Orsay it is extremely quiet, and feels secluded and very much in its own world.

30 L'Hôtel de Sers

34 41, avenue Pierre 1er de Serbie, 8th
Rooms from €450

Tucked away from the frenzy of the Champs-Élysées, the seamless, laser-etched sliding glass doors welcome you to the former *pied à terre* of the Marquis de Sers, a 19th-century townhouse brought forward into the 21st with all the elegance of its Second Empire beginnings. The period interiors have been left open and uncluttered in architect Thomas Vidalenc's design for this new (opened 2004), privately owned hotel. Sitting happily near the border of the 16th arrondissement, it gives easy access to the Eiffel Tower and attractions farther afield such as the Palais de Tokyo (p. 39) and the Bois de Boulogne, while still being centrally oriented toward the luxe shopping and dining of the 8th.

Inside the soaring stone, chandelier-hung entrance, a cerise ribbon of carpet welcomes guests up the stairs to the light, high-ceilinged lounge, where there is an open bar from tea time until 1 am. Downstairs is a bright, modern restaurant serving gastronomic French cuisine at lunch and dinner, and a plant-lined patio garden with ample wood seating. Fifty-two rooms are arranged over eight floors with two panoramic and four junior suites of 40 square metres. The panoramic suites take in a stunning view of the Eiffel Tower, the Arc de Triomphe, and other splendours of the Parisian skyline. Suites have partially enclosed, stepped-up terraces that overhang the placid private garden. The generally white interiors avoid being stark with the use of polished rosewood furnishings, gauzy draperies and a few boldly coloured touches. Clean white, dark wood, stone and bright-red combine throughout to create a style of embellished minimalism, in which you know from the first step through the door that there is a great degree of luxury on offer. Sitting in the neighbourhood of flagship stores for high-end shops like Balenciaga and Jean Paul Gaultier (p. 42), as well as the glamour that surrounds the Champs-Élysées, L'Hôtel de Sers manages to fit right in without announcing itself too proudly. Its glamour is to be found on the inside.

62 L'Hôtel Particulier de Montmartre

24 23, avenue Junot, 18th
Rooms from €390

Opened in 2007, this hidden luxury townhouse hotel is located, it says, 'in the heart of historical Montmartre', but this is well away from the rabble of touristy Montmartre and has all the style of a cultured patron of the visual arts rather than the rather tired legacy of artistic license that many still associate with the quarter. The Directoire-era mansion is set behind an imposing private entrance gate and courtyard garden off a tiny street running between the avenue Junot and the rue Lepic. Owners Morgane Rousseau and Fréderic Comtet and collaborator Mathieu Paillard drew artistic inspiration from those original bohemians – Renoir, Degas, Utrillo, Toulouse-Lautrec – and invited artists currently working in a range of visual media to 'brainstorm' designs for each of the five suites that make up the hotel. These 'apartments' measure 45 to 80 square metres, and are designed around such themes as hip young magazine illustrator Pierre Fichefeux's 'Tree with Ears', which features printed wall decorations in abstractions of trees, luxurious black upholstered furnishings, and gilt-framed mirrors. The 'Vegetal Room' was designed by Martine Aballéa, who enveloped the space in coloured photo prints of trees across the walls and ceiling, which are also accented with coloured lighting. The remaining suites were designed by artist and photographer Natacha Lesueur, Olivier Saillard, events director at the Paris Fashion Museum who titled his room scheme 'Poems and Hats', and painter/sculptor Philippe Mayaux. The common areas have also been appointed with particular style: the Salon, by Finnish designer Mats Haglund, features mid-century classic furnishings by Mies van der Rohe and Arne Jacobsen, while the dining room, which can be used for private dinners, takes a more baroque turn.

Outside, there is a private garden laid out by Louis Bénech, who was in charge of the renovation of the Tuileries, and is a picturesque spot for breakfast or afternoon tea. These luxurious sequestered rooms have accomplished something totally lacking in this area of the city, a truly civilized escape that captures some of the inspiration and beauty that once held a generation of artists in thrall.

GOTHIC REVIVAL REVISITED

78
Hôtel Bourg Tibourg

18

19, rue du Bourg-Tibourg, 4th
Rooms from €200

A crushed velvet-lined lift, striped silk-covered walls, a forest of textures and colours wrapped, draped, gathered and set off with silky fringes – so much dramatic embellishment packed into such a small scale, but that is very much part of the cosy charm of the Hôtel Bourg Tibourg. Paris's pre-eminent design family, the Costes, have pulled out all the stops in their thirty-one-room hotel, formerly the Rivoli Notre Dame, in the heart of the Marais. Famed designer Jacques Garcia has combined Gothic, Oriental, French Empire and a bit of Victorian to ensure that this is an intimate hotel experience that will leave a lasting visual and sensual impression. Every room is a unique pleasure, with beds draped in dark-coloured taffeta or silk, complete with giant tassels. Low lighting and deep hues give the rooms the feeling of a richly appointed medieval garret or the tent of a desert prince. The castle theme is even more apparent in the cellar breakfast room with its stone walls covered with old tapestries and red velvet curtains. Here, in some of the most atmospheric surroundings Paris has to offer, you can also enjoy a candlelit drink, play a game of chess, or retreat up the winding blue-walled staircase to the plush comforts of your room, which is rather anachronistically equipped with an Internet connection. A small garden, designed by Camille Muller, extends the richness out of doors.

None of the extravagance will surprise those who have had the chance to visit another collaboration between the Costes brothers and Garcia, the Hôtel Costes (p. 158), but it is the difference in scale that makes the rue du Bourg-Tibourg's embrace all the more alluring. Although there's no restaurant, you are in the heart of the Marais, a district packed with restaurants, bars and ambience. Try dinner at Au Bourguignon du Marais (p. 85), or book ahead for a truly unforgettable experience at L'Ambroisie (p. 138).

62 **Hôtel Amour**

10 8, rue Navarin, 9th
Rooms from €90

The Hôtel Amour became an instant hit with the arty crowd when it was opened by a team of hip Paris art-scene entrepreneurs that included graffiti artist André (also responsible for popular nightclub Paris Paris). Located in an area full of new and repopulated cafés and clubs, it is one of the prime movers leading the Pigalle in a period of popular and creative rebirth. This is low-budget bohemian with a good dose of style. On arrival guests must wend their way through the inviting and very popular ground-floor café, which is buzzing most times and days of the week, as well as having a lovely walled patio garden. You then take the petite lift (which can accommodate four people at most) to the black-painted hallways leading to the twenty comfortable, inspired rooms, some painted bright-red and all decorated by André or other Parisian artists, including high-demand design duo M/M. Rooms are fairly compact, but big on design touches, such as classic modern furnishings and select pieces of art, including photographs by Terry Richardson. Some rooms have the bath incorporated into the bedroom, surrounded by funky 'métro' tiles, or with free-standing, claw-footed tubs (how romantic is that?); others have them 'hidden' behind sliding doors.

There aren't any grand gestures, phones, Internet or wireless connections, but that's all part of the appeal of a place that, until this renovation, was devoted to more hurried encounters than artful *amour*. With its mix of youthful zest, modern streetwise style and hints of glamour, the Hôtel Amour seems to be what the 9th has been waiting for to inspire its upward turn. Staff are young, groovy and eager to please. The overall feeling is one of good cheer and an attempt to recapture a spirit of creative *je ne sais quois* that's more about how a place makes you feel than what it makes you pay for. Find more cafés and bars on the nearby rue des Martyrs (p. 67).

78 **Murano Urban Resort**
37 13, boulevard du Temple, 3rd
Rooms from €350

The name refers to the Venetian island, not because of all the Murano mirrors, glass and chandeliers, but because of the intention to create an 'island' in the middle of Paris, a secluded world of luxury floating between the *bijoux* streets of the Marais and the gritty street style of the République. Director Jérôme Foucaud comes from a family of hoteliers and left the Byblos hotel group to create this, 'Paris's first urban resort', which opened in 2004. From your first glimpse through the sliding-glass doors past the gleaming white, glass-roofed entrance into the rich red dining room, you'll see that no spot has been overlooked in this Austin-Powers-meets-Space-Odyssey design scheme worked by Christine Derory and Raymond Morel. Even the lift hasn't escaped the colourists: a textured bright faux fur currently engulfs you, but next week it might be zebra-patterned, as the designers like to keep Murano guests guessing.

Guests can also surprise themselves by changing the lighting scheme and colour in their own rooms, which are primarily decked in pure white, with big, bold floral motifs, pieces of Pop Art, and bright modern design objects to keep up with the cutting-edge creative types who stay here. There are twenty-three rooms and nine suites stacked up and around the courtyard bar space, including two *suites de luxe* that feature private swimming pools, defiantly cantilevered over the courtyard but screened by frosted glass. Not for the faint-hearted, and neither are the prices, but the Murano Urban Resort is offering a holistic luxury experience, further enhanced by the basement spa facilities and a notable restaurant under the direction of Pierre Auge, formerly of Sketch in London, and Julien Chicoisne, which has a fine focus on healthy and vegetarian dishes. In its aim to present an atmosphere that is 'chic and relaxed', the Murano is on target with seemingly effortless attention to detail and friendly, accommodating staff who are amazingly unfazed by their place in one of Paris's most fashionable design hotels.

30 **Hôtel Daniel**

50 8, rue Fréderic Bastiat, 8th

Rooms from €330

On a quiet little side street well away from the scrum of the Champs-Élysées, but still redolent with the glitter of the 8th, the Hôtel Daniel has been around for years but had its glamour reawakened with a wholesale refurbishment in 2004, after which it was invited to become a member of Relais & Châteaux. Keen to steer clear of global corporate minimalism, the hotel's owner granted designer Tarfa Salam free rein to rework the interiors in a way that would 'stimulate the imagination' and retain something of the intimacy of a private house. The result is a sumptuous recreation of the French 18th-century *chinoiserie* and 'near Eastern' style. Antiques and period buffs will marvel at the mixture of 18th-century furnishings and studious re-creations, such as the inlaid tables, mosaic mirrors, hand-painted wallpapers and the *toile de jouy* used generously throughout the public and private spaces, while the romantic traveller will revel in the luxurious mix of patterns, colours and textures of the ample draperies and plush upholstery all inspired by the idea of 'a journey along the Silk Road as seen by the 18th-century French traveller.'

There are twenty-six rooms (including nine suites), and each is decorated in different mixtures of patterns and colours, with specially designed wallpaper printed in either *chinoiserie* or period French pastoral motifs, *toile de jouy*, plump upholstered sofas, hand-crafted wood furniture, and an array of artworks and artefacts. Bathrooms are tiled in *zellige* (Moroccan ceramics) or Italian marble, and stocked with Dead Sea bath salts and soaps hand-made in Lebanon. Rooms on the second and fifth floors have private balconies, and the sixth-floor rooms under the eaves are popular as the angled portion of the roof is glass, allowing for fantastic city views. The ground-floor lounge, where guests can enjoy cocktails or afternoon tea, is a sumptuous den of decorative riches with hand-painted wallcoverings, furniture and other pieces specially created by French artisans, who also contributed to the intimate dining room. Classically trained chef Denis Fetisson runs the gourmet restaurant and also blends East and West. The kitchen offers an 'all-day breakfast' that includes pastries by Ladurée.

14 **L'Hôtel**

13, rue des Beaux-Arts, 6th
Rooms from €280

Dramatic, luxurious, historic and with a fabulous location in the heart of St-Germain-des-Prés, L'Hôtel is a complete experience in the way that a small luxury hotel should be. Its Directoire period elements have been meticulously restored down to the last plaster detail in the neoclassically inspired cupola, which rises up to a spectacular skylit height, with galleried walkways overlooking the hall from all six floors. The themed bedrooms have plush combinations of the fabrics and furniture for which designer Jacques Garcia has become famous, and he has lavished the same treatment on the public rooms. The restaurant is full of swags and mirrors, period pendant lamps, a fountain and thickly upholstered seating in bohemian red patterns and crisp striped taffeta. Oscar Wilde, who died in the hotel in 1900, has a room dedicated to his luxurious tastes, with some touches of his Irish provenance and letters from him scattered throughout (as well as letters to him asking for payment of debts). If the hotel was anything as wonderful then as it is today, his famous last words, 'I shall have to die above my means', are easily understood. The room labelled 'Mistinguett' is an essay in Art Déco, with plenty of boldly coloured velvet and streamlined decorative objects honouring the singer's heyday in Paris. Other rooms – the 'Marco Polo', the 'St Petersburg', the 'Pompéienne', the 'Reine Hortense' – are decorated in similarly extravagant fashion. The 'Cardinal' is particularly provocative in varying shades of purple.

A hotel since 1825, the recent incarnation is only a few years old and gives the place real star quality. The once-abandoned underground cellar has been reclaimed and now houses a tiled sauna and intimate swimming pool, lit by candelabra on the walls and, if you like, surrounded by tea lights. Two bars have been decked out in Garcia's Belle Époque fantasy dressing, like the restaurant, Le Bélier, where the cuisine is well prepared with a small and well-considered wine list.

78 FASHIONABLE RETREAT

9 3Rooms

5, rue de Moussy, 4th

Apartments from €400

He doesn't advertise and there isn't any brochure, but *haute couture* designer Azzedine Alaïa hasn't had any trouble getting people to sample his new venture into élite Parisian accommodation. Having converted a 17th-century building near his loft-like boutique (p. 175) in the Marais into three separate apartments, Alaïa maintains the same understated, non-branded approach as he does with his artfully arranged retail space: no banners, no lighted sign, just a simple address and phone number opens the gate to his world of refined living. The design for each apartment was conceived by Alaïa himself, and each is furnished in modern and Modernist style with pieces from the designer's own private collection. The furnishings by Jean Prouvé, Jean Nouvel and Arne Jacobsen, objects by Marc Newson and lighting fixtures by Serge Mouille make you feel as if you are in your own private design haven in the centre of Paris, at least for a while. Floor-to-ceiling windows make the already airy white spaces lighter and brighter. Each 100-square metre apartment is fully self-contained with complete kitchen facilities, so clients from fashion models to conscientious weight-watchers can create cuisine to their own specific requirements, or just make their own coffee and keep the wine chilled.

Opened only in 2004, Alaïa's fashionable home away from home has already proved a hit, especially during fashion and media events. But mere mortals can still reserve by telephone or email. Two apartments have a double and single bedroom, while the third is a one-bedroom. Prices include breakfast, and other meals, when not prepared *à la maison*, can be easily sourced in the many Marais eateries. Wander over for a drink on top of the Centre Pompidou (p. 80), allow a gastronomic indulgence at Au Bourguignon du Marais (p. 85), perhaps, or sink into the sheer splendour of L'Ambroisie (p. 138) in the nearby place des Vosges.

eat

Thanks to falling prices and a new generation of chefs, Paris has recently, and rather swiftly, become a less expensive, less intimidating, more informal and more open culinary destination. Many young chefs promote what food writers call 'bistronomic' venues, which feature great food in a laid-back atmosphere. For those wishing to experience (and have remembered to book before travelling) the apotheosis of gastronomy, Paris remains unrivalled: Alain Ducasse at the Plaza Athénée, Jean-François Piège at the Crillon, Pierre Gagnaire and Joël Robuchon offer once-in-a-lifetime pleasures. Don't forget the family-run bistros, the essence of everyday cooking, which continue to thrive and reinvent themselves.

Guy Savoy

37 18, rue Troyon, 17th

A lover of the arts and fashion, Guy Savoy likes to say
that his restaurant, recently redecorated by Jean-Michel
Wilmotte (with dark African wood, beige leather and
modern paintings), is nothing but a 21st-century inn —
in so saying he has described in a nutshell the warmth and
casualness he promotes in this exceptional establishment.
And it is noteworthy that the excellent staff offer something
different (with cheerful greetings and other attentive
details, such as the placing of a napkin on your knees) and
that the atmosphere is much more relaxed than in other
such places. The food manages to be something between
true luxury and false simplicity, with the artichoke and
black truffle *velouté* as bridgehead. It is quite often amazing,
especially with the help of sommelier Eric Mancio, one
of Paris's most renowned professionals.

THE CRITICS' BISTRO
46 **Chez Georges**
40 1, rue du Mail, 2nd

Asked to name their favourite bistro, many of Paris's sharpest food writers choose Chez Georges (not to be confused with the restaurant on top of the Centre Pompidou; p. 80). When you stand before the tiny wooden façade, you may wonder why, for the place looks like many others. But walk in, sit down, and you'll understand what a perfect traditional bistro should look like. First, it has to do with the atmosphere, which is so French and old-fashioned you might think you've travelled back to the 1960s: an elegant though unpretentious dining room with one long, white-tableclothed stretch of tables between the mirrored walls. For food, you'll enjoy perfect herrings, foie gras, *andouillettes, petit salé*, steaks and perhaps the best French fries in the city. The wine list veers towards the expensive, though that in no way diminishes Chez Georges's timeless appeal.

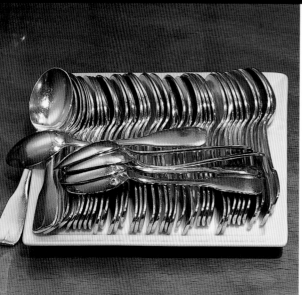

30 La Table du Joël Robuchon

30 16, avenue Bugeaud, 16th

A number of food critics decidedly favour this, Joël Robuchon's second restaurant, serving smaller portions in a less formal atmosphere, over his much-publicized L'Atelier in the 7th (5–7, rue de Montalembert). Why is that? Firstly – *impossible n'est pas français* – you can actually book a table here, which, believe it or not, simply can't be done at L'Atelier (unless you're willing to eat your lunch at 11.30 am). Secondly, there is a brilliant pastry chef at La Table, whose imagination stretches well beyond the familiar répertoire of fruit tarts. And finally, while the classic food (thyme-flavoured lamb, fried whiting, to name just a few) strikes just the right chord, the sommelier offers about twenty different wines by the glass, enabling you to dine accompanied by a Latour 1990, without having to buy the full bottle.

Le Grand Véfour

21 17, rue de Beaujolais, 1st

Would Victor Hugo still recognize 'his' restaurant? Certainly, though in his time it was still called 'Le Café de Chartres'. Originally built in 1784, what was to become Le Grand Véfour has welcomed absolutely everybody, from Napoleon to Colette and Jean Cocteau – most seats bear a small brass plaque commemorating some famous patron. In those days, it was probably the most beautiful restaurant in Paris and today it probably still is, mostly because it is charged with so much history and so exquisitely adorned. Against the opulent surroundings, chef Guy Martin's food has a contemporary feel, blending sophistication and rusticity. He hails from the mountains of Savoie, so you'll find earthy dishes among all the foie gras, truffle-stuffed ravioli, or the famous artichoke pie (a dessert).

Gallopin

23 40, rue Notre-Dame-des-Victoires, 2nd

Next to the old stock exchange, Gallopin has long been a headquarters for the brokers and journalists who work nearby. But it is mainly one of the city's most beautiful brasseries, with an ageless 1880s décor (superb mahogany panelling, mirrors, glass roof, brass lamps, and a bar for those who just want to read a newspaper), originally created by Gustave Gallopin for his establishment in London (his wife was English), the Stock Exchange Luncheon Bar, but now adorns its Paris reincarnation. Regulars say that it is impossible to find a more Parisian place than this. Food is as traditional as you can imagine, which means that you can enjoy dipping into a huge seafood platter before indulging in some hot *crêpes Suzette,* naturally sprinkled with Grand Marnier and set alight in front of you. Magic, eternal, unique.

ÉLÉGANCE SUPRÈME

78 **L'Ambroisie**

17 9, place des Vosges, 4th

If you are fond of food, you will most probably have heard of chefs like Alain Ducasse (see p. 147) or Bernard Loiseau, from Burgundy. But does the name of Bernard Pacaud ring a bell? If not, you don't know what you've been missing. This very discreet man runs one of the city's best restaurants – some would even say *the* best restaurant – set in one of Paris's best locations. The moment you arrive under the magnificent arcades of the 17th-century place des Vosges and step into the hushed elegance of the Viennese-inflected interior designed by François-Joseph Graf, you begin to get a sense of what makes this place so special. L'Ambroisie is simply the epitome of classic French cuisine, but with a twist of modernity. Sharp flavours, high prices, a truly memorable experience. Like at L'Astrance (see left), reservations should be made at least one month in advance.

SMALL BUT PERFECTLY FORMED

30 **L'Astrance**

20 4, rue Beethoven, 16th

It was something like love at first sight. When chef Pascal Barbot and maître d' Christophe Rohat (both formerly at Alain Passard's restaurant, L'Arpège; p. 144) opened their tiny (fewer than a dozen tables), elegant restaurant in 2001, every single food lover in Paris begged for a table. L'Astrance, named after a flower from Auvergne, instantly became the city's best newcomer for years, with its modern, creative and sharp cooking (avocado and crab ravioli is one of their most famous dishes). Make sure to let them handle your meal and you'll most certainly have a great time. Adopt the same attitude with wines: Monsieur Rohat knows best. Reservations should be made at least one month in advance.

THE SWEDISH CHEF

98 La Gazzetta

9 29, rue de Cotte, 12th

Swedish native Peter Nilsson practises chefdom in the heart of the trendy Bastille, and from the name of his restaurant you'd expect pizza and pasta galore. But La Gazzetta really stands out. Nilsson adds kuri squash, walnuts and yoghurt to his risotto, salt-preserved lemon, quinoa and cauliflower to his lamb short ribs, and grapefruit, tarragon and leeks to his scallops. An unexpected and delicious experience, set within a décor that is half-brasserie, half-bistro.

62

Senderens

3 9, place de la Madeleine, 8th

Alain Senderens, who used to be the high priest of *nouvelle cuisine*, created a sensation two years ago by publicly announcing that he was giving away the three Michelin stars earned by his restaurant, Lucas-Carton. His 'new' restaurant — simply renamed 'Senderens' — still holds on to two stars, but the prices have been divided by three. Quite a good reason to pay a new visit to the place, as is the sublime Art Nouveau dining room, artfully updated by a young interior designer in a style that constantly oscillates between classical and neo-futuristic. On the menu, the chef dares to replace costly turbot with cheap and delicious sardines (stuffed Moroccan-style with rice, herbs and spices), the chicken is from Challans (and the vegetables cooked with truffles), and the crumble pudding prepared with coconut. The wine and food pairings are just as fabulous as ever.

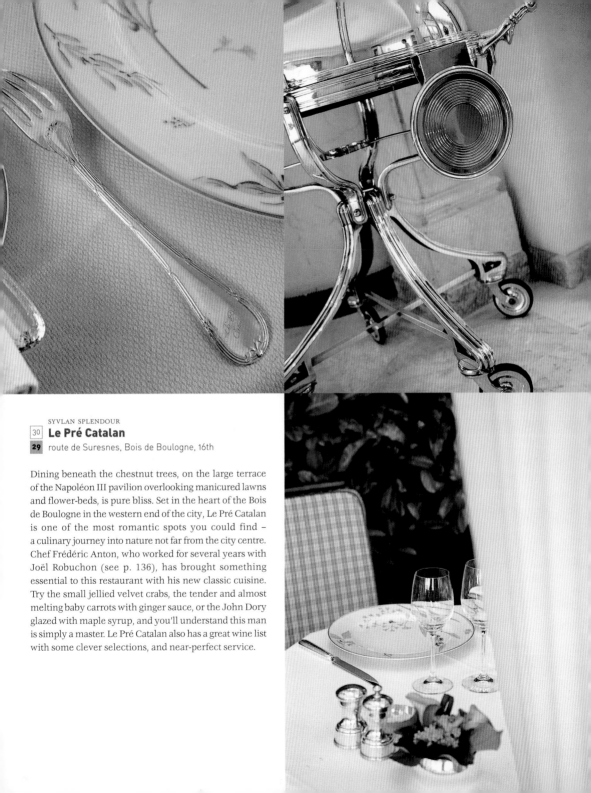

30 **Le Pré Catalan**

29 route de Suresnes, Bois de Boulogne, 16th

Dining beneath the chestnut trees, on the large terrace of the Napoléon III pavilion overlooking manicured lawns and flower-beds, is pure bliss. Set in the heart of the Bois de Boulogne in the western end of the city, Le Pré Catalan is one of the most romantic spots you could find – a culinary journey into nature not far from the city centre. Chef Frédéric Anton, who worked for several years with Joël Robuchon (see p. 136), has brought something essential to this restaurant with his new classic cuisine. Try the small jellied velvet crabs, the tender and almost melting baby carrots with ginger sauce, or the John Dory glazed with maple syrup, and you'll understand this man is simply a master. Le Pré Catalan also has a great wine list with some clever selections, and near-perfect service.

NEIGHBOURHOOD STAR

98 Le Villaret

24 13, rue Ternaux, 11th

What used to be a fabulous neighbourhood bistro with clever cooking is becoming, year after year, a truly ambitious restaurant (in the positive sense of the word). But new visitors needn't worry, the overall style hasn't changed at all: Le Villaret still has a laid-back atmosphere and a funky clientele, with its strange mix of young hipsters, grannies from next door, wine lovers ordering five bottles at a time (the wine list is constantly improving) and businessmen in white collars with loosened ties. Though prices have risen in recent years, the place still draws numerous patrons (reservations essential), who know that quality and taste will be part of the deal. Self-taught chef Olivier Gaslain likes tweaking classic French cooking, though there's little likelihood you will bump into a Camembert pizza or other such fusion silliness here. It also benefits from being open until very late at night.

SURPRISING DELIGHTS

30 Pierre Gagnaire

38 Hôtel Balzac, 6, rue Balzac, 8th

Forget saying 'I do not remember ordering this' when the staff bring six or seven small dishes to your table, that's just the beginning of every meal at Pierre Gagnaire. Wildly creative tapas are offered as a kind of welcome present, to give you a first glimpse of Gagnaire's kind of cooking. Poetic, sincere, intuitive and spontaneous, he is also capable of surprising even those who are frequent visitors to this modern grey-painted and wood-clad dining room. One can never tell what a meal will be like here, as Gagnaire sometimes changes his menus or his recipes on the same day that he presents them. All you need to know is that his cooking often blends unexpected flavours, textures and products. Just let the staff handle your journey; it could very well be an unforgettable one.

THE TASTE OF INSPIRATION
30 La Table du Lancaster
43 Hôtel Lancaster, 7, rue de Berri, 8th

'The wit of tomato', 'the brightness of lemon and citrus fruit', 'the piquancy of spices and condiments', 'the sharpness of vegetables, herbs and fruit', 'the sourness of dairy products': all you need to grasp the novelty of Michel Troisgros's approach to cooking is to read the headings on the menu at this, his first Parisian spot. Upon taking over the kitchen at the exclusive, almost secluded Hôtel Lancaster , the three-starred chef (based in Roanne) chose to show off his brilliant cuisine at its lightest and shrewdest. Once you've tasted his food, be it Japanese *koshi-hikari* rice in a cod broth, veal's liver with almonds and red currants, or the amazing tamarind frog's legs, you'll know the hotelier made a clever move when trusting Troisgros with the revamping of his restaurant.

SEASONAL PLEASURES
14 La Régalade
31 49, avenue Jean-Moulin, 14th

Succeeding Yves Camdeborde, whose time at La Régalade was hailed as a gastronomic achievement, was always going to be a challenge. Fortunately, against all odds, Bruno Doucet took it up and carried it off brilliantly. To begin with, he chose not to touch the décor created by his predecessor and managed to avoid a complete turnover of staff. In the kitchen, he simply kept things just as they used to be. So, quite simply, the mood hasn't changed a bit and we're all as happy as ever to travel deep into the 14th arrondissement to enjoy a fun, friendly, noisy and lively evening. The menu features subtly classic seasonal dishes such as sautéed cep mushrooms, veal's liver, whole roasted foie gras, and, during winter, outstanding game. Nothing to add, except that the place continues to stand out as the essential modern bistro.

30 L'Arpège

Even Alain Passard's biggest fans will tell you his restaurant
is one of the most expensive in Paris: the exciting but for
many almost unattainable *menu dégustation* is to blame,
as is the ambitious wine list. But if money is no object, and
you find yourself hungry after a stroll around the Musée
Rodin, L'Arpège is definitely a must-visit, particularly
if you have vegetarian inclinations. Passard decided
a couple of years ago to focus on vegetables, which he
grows in his personal garden in Anjou (but he also serves
seafood and poultry). Try the sweet onions with Parmesan
and black pepper, little beets with a syrupy balsamic
vinegar and black truffles, or a carrot and verbena
consommé; you'll feel as if you've never tasted vegetables
before. A captivating, bold and unique gastronomic
experience, worth every Euro.

14 Ze Kitchen Galerie

Those who have travelled the world might feel they've seen
something quite similar in other global capitals – five
years ago. But a place like Ze Kitchen Galerie in Paris
is something new: it has a Modernist, white-washed loft-
like décor, paintings on the walls and an open kitchen
you can freely peer into through a glass panel
(a genuine novelty in the city). Located in the 6th
arrondissement's high concentration of antiques and
furniture galleries, it has a relaxed and peaceful
atmosphere. The food created by chef William Ledeuil
complements this mood with a vocabulary of its own:
playful, sharp, quick-paced and open-minded (plenty
of Asian herbs and spices), with a destructured *carte*,
allowing one to choose pasta and soup instead of the
traditional starter followed by main course followed
by dessert. Marinated raw fish, meats or vegetables *à la
planche*, creative desserts: an artful place, an artful location,
an artful chef – worth many visits.

98 Le Chateaubriand

26 129, avenue Parmentier, 11th

Belgian endive, darkened from a lengthy roasting, its bitterness balanced by the acidic tones of a citrus salad and rounded off by the sweetness of powdered gingerbread; pure white squid meat served on top of an ink-black stew made from the tentacles; lamb saddle paired with a small quantity of horseradish and smoked haddock and served with an incredibly smooth sweet potato purée: those were just a few of young chef Inaki Aizpitarte's many palatable, bistro-chic ideas. Womens' magazines worship him, but they are not alone. Foodies from San Francisco, Tokyo, Bangkok and Brooklyn equally adore him. On top of all this, the place is a lovely 1930s restaurant, set in one of the coolest neighbourhoods in Paris.

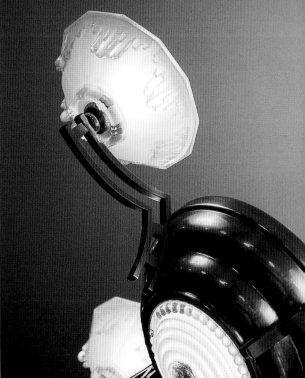

30 **The Cristal Room**

31 11, place des États-Unis, 16th

Will star designer Philippe Starck ever become boring? His knack of coming up with brilliant ideas whenever working on a new project makes it hard to believe. The atmosphere at The Cristal Room, embedded in Baccarat's headquarters, is simply unique in a poetic and often funny way – does *Alice in Wonderland* ring a bell? Indeed, don't miss the huge chandeliers, the black-and-pink boudoir, the giant-sized chairs, the brick walls, the 15- metre-long showroom table. In a nutshell, a clever layout that brings back to life the surreal and extravagant spirit of Marie-Laure de Noailles, former lady of the house and friend of Cocteau, Dalí, Buñuel and Man Ray. The cooking is no less imaginative, involving 'fleeting' ravioli of oyster, a citrus-flavoured *sole meunière*, or quince and apples served with a frosted lolly. All this comes at a price, a mile-high price. But you can visit the museum for a nominal sum and perhaps treat yourself to a slightly less extravagant lunch or afternoon tea.

GRAND PERFECTION
30 Alain Ducasse au Plaza Athénée
45 Hôtel Plaza Athénée, 25, avenue Montaigne, 8th

'French excellence': Alain Ducasse's catchphrase is ultimately quite simple. And how does the country's star chef manage to maintain such a standard? He simply chooses the best money can buy (from salt to butter, lobster to lamb, poultry to asparagus, and one of the few restaurants in Paris where you can taste the horrendously expensive Italian white truffle in winter), hired the best staff one can imagine (from chef to sommeliers, maître d's to waiters), and asked young designer Patrick Jouin to create what is currently one of the most surprising décors of such upper-class venues (Louis XV-style chairs, painted gunmetal-grey, combined with modern touches such as the holographic lighting effects produced by a huge organza veil). Such perfection is hard to find.

HIGH TABLE
30 Les Ambassadeurs
15 Hôtel de Crillon, 10, place de la Concorde, 8th

The arrival of Jean-François Piège at Les Ambassadeurs after many years spent under the coaching of Alain Ducasse (see left) was, according to some, no less significant and expensive than a football transfer. As a result, the young chef has become sole master-of-command on board a magnificent 18th-century dining room reminiscent of the famous *galerie des glaces* in Versailles. Tons of crystal, luxurious wall hangings, a view over the place de la Concorde, staff clad in black uniforms (specially cut to give a new twist to old-school style), and shocking bills: you'll quickly grasp the fact that an evening here is extra-special occasion material. Young pigeon with foie gras and olives, crayfish in a spicy broth, or Bresse poultry accompanied by spaghetti carbonara are washed down with equally exceptional wines. A living proof of how the shape of tomorrow's French classic cuisine is being designed by a crop of creative young chefs.

drink

Going out for a drink in Paris is an experience you'll find hard to match in almost any other city in the world. In the land of the *flâneur*, it is about using your eyes and ears as much as your palate, for the best drinking spots are steeped in the French sensitivity to beauty, style and ambience. Romantic images of Parisian café society, as clichéd as they have become, are not entirely untrue. From grand Belle Époque hotel bars to the latest designer restaurant space, funky revival cafés to revered neighbourhood establishments, cocktails and wine to coffee and tea, the places where Parisians (and lucky foreigners) go to sit and sip and look and listen cover a range of moods and moments — always with panache.

HAMMAM AND MINT TEA
14 La Mosquée de Paris
■ 39, rue Geoffroy-St-Hilaire, 5th

If you're planning a visit to the spectacular Jardin des Plantes, then it's also a good time to take in the 1920s mosque built in Hispano-Moorish style by three French architects and decorated by numerous North African artisans. Featuring lacy Moorish patterns in intricately carved wood screens, decorative tilework and lighting and ornate cupolas, the mosque also has beautifully kept patio gardens. You might enjoy the hammam or have traditional mint tea at the café/tea room in a plant-filled courtyard, itself reminiscent of a Mughal palace.

SPLENDID SETTING
46 Le Saut du Loup
7 107, rue de Rivoli, 1st

The ten-year renovation project of the Musée des Arts Décoratifs (p. 49) also brought this new restaurant designed with sexy black-and-white interiors by Philippe Boisselier and menu by decorator-turned-chef Pascal Bernier, who serves up three-patty-tall hamburger towers as well as more delicate dishes. But for real ambience go for a table outside where you can sit in garden splendour between the Carousel du Louvre at one end of the vista and the Tuileries at the other. The food quality is changeable, so order a *café crème* or a cup of tea and an indulgent ice-cream dessert, or a glass of wine, anything really to keep a seat in what has been named 'the most beautiful terrace in Paris'.

30 **15cent15**

48 Hôtel Marignan, 12, rue Marignan, 8th

The frustrating lack of stylish bars that aren't filled with hordes of noisy trawlers around the Champs-Élysées is one reason why the recent makeover of the Marignan's lounge bar by Olivier Gagnère is such a welcome change. Luxurious seating, soft brown wallcovering, taffeta drapery and Murano chandeliers are all very 21st-century Paris, but no less appealing for it. The cocktail list is good, the music not too thunderous, and the whole mix attracts a pleasantly stylish crowd in the evenings, but it's also a quiet spot for a late afternoon bit of well-mannered calm.

FUGITIVE OENOPHILIA
78 **Le Verre Volé**
39 67, rue de Lancry, 10th

Wine bar, wine shop and micro-bistro rolled into one: this is what makes 'the stolen glass' such an unusual place. Since the word has begun to spread out of the Canal St-Martin area and across Paris, you'll need to book one of the four or five tables if you want to eat or be seated to enjoy some of the finest wines of the moment (the white Côteaux d'Aix-en-Provence from Château Bas, the Vinsobres from the Domaine Gramenon in the Rhône valley) with a simple plate of cheese or oysters. The tiny locale doesn't inhibit enjoyment, however – it can be wild from time to time.

CLASSIC WINE SHOP
46 **Legrand Filles et Fils**
25 1, rue de la Banque, 2nd

When you enter you're bound to spend the first hour simply admiring the place. Legrand Filles et Fils is pure beauty, one of Paris's oldest *épiceries fines*, run by the same family for decades. Consider the candies, the ports, the dozens of wines, then grab a seat at the bar, which is in the brand-new area of the store. If you want to discover some great wines, just ask for one of the fifteen served by the glass, from Sancerre to Chilean Cabernet-Sauvignon. Food? Pleasing plates of goat's cheese, charcuteries or foie gras, all from the best producers in the country.

Caves Miard
9, rue des Quatre-Vents, 6th

Le Baratin
27 3, rue Jouye-Rouve, 20th

Yes, another restaurant and shop. Yet you should take a closer look – the place is simply beautiful. Picture a seventy-year-old ham slicer set in a splendidly preserved 19th-century décor. Imagine top-of-the-crop wines, at their unsulphured, healthy and nature-friendly best. Add a charming young owner wearing a funky cap, and top it all off with exceptional Italian cured meats (such as *culatello*, *coppa* or *lardo di Colonnata*). And now you'll understand why the few tables are constantly taken over by a pool of enthusiastic customers.

Take no notice if you hear a Spanish-accented woman's voice yelling from the kitchen: that's Raquel, the cook, from Argentina. Le Baratin (French for 'jive') is one of Belleville's most famous wine bars: unexpected, unusual, bohemian and engaging – definitely the place to go if you want to grasp something of the eastern Parisian state of mind. Don't forget to book a table (the place is always full and smoky) to try one of the numerous wines by the glass (the wine list is remarkable) and one of Raquel's Franco-Argentinian dishes.

TEA CEREMONIES

14 **La Maison des Trois Thés**

33, rue Gracieuse, 5th

Tea is becoming more popular in Paris, though, as you might expect, in a refined and sometimes even *haute* manner. At La Maison des Trois Thés, Taiwanese proprietress Yu Hui Tseng, one of the leading tea-masters in the world and an official expert for the Chinese government, is on a mission to promote the ancient *gong fu* ceremony in Europe, along with a genuine appreciation of tea. Offering more than a thousand varieties of teas, from the humble jasmine to the rare (and dear) oolong, her tea house has the largest selection in the world, but the setting is pleasantly intimate, modern and serene.

Some, even some Parisians, describe this bar as the most beautiful in Paris. Beneath Murano glass chandeliers, grey Louis XV-style stools line the long, transparent bar that glows like a slab of blue ice. The décor is the work of Patrick Jouin, who redid the interior after the bar was destroyed by fire in 2000 – one reason, perhaps, for the icy feel. The wood panelling and chandeliers survived, and the stage was set for the models, actresses and rock stars who like to lounge and revel in its glory. Sip a Champagne Mojito and watch the limousines arrive; save the jelly shots for later.

OLD-STYLE ELEGANCE
30 Le Dokhan's
24 Hôtel Sofitel, 117, rue Lauriston, 16th

Billed as Paris's only Champagne bar, Le Dokhan's is on the
ground floor of the Haussmann-era Hôtel Sofitel, renovated
in 2006. The richly embellished interiors were the work
of Frédéric Méchiche, with glittering chandeliers and
hung with miles of taffeta drapery. A different Champagne
is served each week, though you can choose between
vintages and degrees of sec (along with your preferred style
of glass). A quiet spot for a romantic pre-dinner drink on
your way to Joël Robuchon (p. 136) or L'Astrance (p. 138),
or to round off your evening, as it's open until 2 am.

CLUB STYLE
62 | Sous les Joups
22 12, rue Durantin, 18th

Nightclub entrepreneur Reynald opened this small but
lovingly formed bar that is a throwback to the days of
chrome and curves, but is very much in the now, with cool
coloured lighting and a vibrant groove later in the evening.
The cocktail list and service are much better than you
might expect from a place that goes for a late-night crowd,
but it's a perfect place to stop for an early evening drink on
the quiet rue Durantin, just far enough away from the
Montmartre crowds to feel a little bit like a local. Look for
the name in bright-red bulbs, and for the many group
events when Reynald partners with some of Paris's best
clubs and bars to present special events and performances.

FAR OUT, BABY

78 Murano Urban Resort Bar

13, boulevard du Temple, 3rd

You may feel the need to utter something about 'Bond' when you walk in the door of this fun and futuristic watering hole set in the ultra-mod lobby of the new hotel (p. 124). As if the shiny white space, complete with white Chesterfield sitting nonchalantly near the block fireplace isn't chic enough, the bar, with walls upholstered in fuchsia and plum, zinc tables and stools and a range of 100 types of vodka, signals a new high in decadent drinking. In the early evening piano music provides a civilizing touch, while later on the DJs take over to add vibe to vibrancy.

SECOND-EMPIRE SEDUCTION

46 Hôtel Costes

2 239, rue St-Honoré, 1st

It's been described as everything from Second Empire bordello to just plain over-the-top, but the Hôtel Costes, designed by Jacques Garcia, has to be seen to be believed. The miles of striped, tasselled, tented and draped fabric, the forest of columns, the lighting and atmosphere is discreet *haute*-meets-hallucinogenic. But despite the décor's exuberance, the tables are all somehow intimate, tucked between columns or nestled beneath the courtyard umbrellas. For drinking in a bit of theatre, Hôtel Costes is a superlative experience.

This new addition to the café-bar-restaurant scene on the
border of the 9th and 10th arrondissements is attracting diners,
drinkers and pre-club hangers-on in droves. The design
by Périphériques swings from cool, orange-and-black plastic
chairs on the deck terrace to the odd geometric forms of the
wood furnishings to candelabra and velvet upholstery. The
ceiling mosaics in the lounge are worthy of a reclining gaze and
may be a holdover from the building's previous incarnation
as a brothel, or some other glimpse of Parisian history. Come
for a drink, stay to watch the crowds.

The family behind the China Club's colonial chic created
Le Fumoir in a similar style, complete with slow-turning
ceiling fans. It's a café, bar and restaurant that combines the
look and feel of a gentleman's club library with a smooth,
1930s-inspired décor. The location is hard to beat, opposite
the cour Carrée du Louvre, with a few tables outside and
some just inside the door, where people lounge and read
the newspaper or the Fumoir's own literary review. The bar
is a great old-fashioned wood-and-mirror affair, a sign of
a serious drinks list, while the restaurant serves a fusion-
style menu. The library is where everyone wants to be, and
any seat you manage to get – and this could prove difficult
– won't disappoint.

shop

In a city that defines style not only in the fickle fashion world but also in furniture and product design, shopping is a near-spiritual experience. Where to begin the quest? Furniture from Louis XV to Jean Michel Franck to Philippe Starck or the newest crop of hip French designers, all available from a host of enthusiastic and knowledgeable dealers? Stunningly attired boutiques that lure you in, whether they're selling *chaussures* or chocolates, perfumes or *patisserie*. The fashion empires of the Champs-Élysées and St-Germain-des-Prés are irresistible, but so are the young, independent craftspeople of the Marais and Montmartre, who produce their handcrafted goods in boutiques where one-off products can be purchased directly from the creator.

46 Van Cleef & Arpels

13 24, place Vendôme, 1st

Having been a globally recognized name for over century, this renowned jewelry store experienced something of a rebirth in 2007 when Patrick Jouin refurbished the premises in what can only be described as a decorative *coup de maître*. Carved wood and gilded walls with bas-relief roses undulate through the shop, and a centre display room is hung with hundreds of delicate Murano glass bubbles. It's like walking onto a film set for a Fred Astaire spectacular – you'll expect the dancers to appear any minute while you contemplate old and new designs that resonate with the glamour of Parisian high society.

CONTEMPORARY CLASSICS

78 Sentou Galerie

12 24, rue du Pont Louis-Philippe, 4th

The Sentou collection made its name under Robert Sentou, who began selling Isamu Noguchi lamps and exhibited the soon-to-be-famous staircase by Roger Tallon. Pierre Romanet, who took over from Sentou in the 1980s, has expanded the range and championed new designers such as Tsé & Tsé and Christian Biecher through stocking their pieces and holding exhibitions. He's now known as a patron of new French design, promoting the work of Frédéric Sofia, Pierre Paulin, Jérôme Gauthier, Robert le Héros and David Design.

PARIS'S OLDEST DEPARTMENT STORE

30 Le Bon Marché

2 24, rue de Sèvres, 7th

Paris's first department store, with metalwork designed by Gustave Eiffel, maintains its *fin-de-siècle* and 1920s decoration. Émile Zola was inspired by its social scene, and it remains one of Paris's most fashionable places to shop. Womens- and menswear sections feature the latest designs, from Gaultier (see pp. 42 and 54) to Galliano, as well as the store's less expensive own brand. Perfume and lingerie departments are brilliantly stocked with those goods for which the French have long been famous. The food hall, or *grande épicerie,* is as grand and beautiful as it is tempting.

SWEET ARTS

14 Pierre Hermé
72, rue Bonaparte, 6th

To know him is to love his creations: melt-in-your-mouth macaroons, apple-and-almond milk tart, 'velvet heart' cake – like beautiful still-lifes that you can eat. All Paris is wild about Pierre Hermé, as you can tell by the queue stretching out of his tiny jewel-box shop designed by Yann Pennor, especially on a Friday afternoon. Uniquely creative with chocolate, Hermé works like a fashion designer, creating 'collections' by season, and has recently opened a tea room off the Champs-Élysées.

BIJOUX PERFUME

46 JAR
4 14, rue de Castiglione, 1st

Exclusive jewelry designer Joel Rosenthal has always had a passion for perfume, to the extent that he started collecting classic scents. He created his first fragrance, Golconda, in the late 1980s, but it was available only in its special Baccarat bottle through selected outlets. In 2001, he launched five more fragrances in this tiny, mauve velvet-wrapped shop, which displays the fragrances and bottles he has designed for them like jewels. Rosenthal intended that the experience would leave the impression of being enveloped by something wonderfully exclusive.

The play of light in Rei Kawakubo's paean to minimalism somehow echoes the subtle, sensual distinctions of scent. Following the success of her Comme des Garçons fashion label (a similarly hard-edged, red shop at 54, rue du Faubourg-St-Honoré), Kawakubo launched five perfumes, which are all displayed here to great effect along white-enamelled steel units. The pink-coloured glass front designed by London's Future Systems changes from opaque to transparent; the colour is taken from the packaging of 'Odeur 71'.

Frédéric Malle wanted to revolutionize perfume-making, so he hired nine reputable *créateurs* and gave them carte blanche to produce original, complex scents. These mystery 'noses', formerly unknown because of their associations with large perfumeries, now have their names attached to the scents created under the auspices of Malle's Editions de Parfums, which he says he produces like a publisher. Interiors were designed by Malle with his friend Andrée Putman, 'the godmother of the shop', together with her protégé, architect Olivier de Lempereur.

GRAND PERFUMERIE AND SPA

30
41 **Guerlain**

68, avenue des Champs-Élysées, 8th

In creating this new space in the company headquarters, designer Andrée Putman and architect Maxime d'Angeac preserved the air of Parisian glamour that Guerlain has maintained for five generations. The original staircase was kept and is backed by a curved gold mosaic tile wall, a fitting ascendance to rooms that house the oldest and most renowned perfumes in bottles created by Raymond Guerlain and Baccarat. In the spa, ten rooms are devoted to beauty treatments and clients are offered a view of one of the most famous streets in the world.

Diane de Montjamont offers bespoke cosmetic services in a grand 18th-century building that still has the wood panelling and parquet flooring that it did when the original owner, an architect to Louis XV, lived here. Make-up artist Hélène Lefur will consult with you in a room with specially designed lighting that re-creates a day or night effect, offering a selection of Poudrier Eternité, made from precious metals, in made-to-measure colour combinations. Your choice is encased in a hand-made compact covered in luxury materials such as Swarovski crystals or crocodile. While you are waiting, enjoy installations commissioned to complement the interiors with a bit of modern design.

46 **Pierre Hardy**

17 Jardins du Palais Royal, 156, galerie de Valois, 1st

What better address than in the arcade of the Palais Royal to show off shoes by fashion royalty. After working with Christian Dior, Hermès and Balenciaga, Pierre Hardy launched his own line in 1999 and entered men's shoe design in 2002. He has opened his first boutique, designed by Ignacio Prego and Jean Bocabeille, to use light and reflection and the contrast qualities of black to showcase his brightly coloured pumps, boots and and evening shoes in dramatic fashion, especially those with metallic heels.

 Christian Louboutin

 19, rue Jean-Jacques-Rousseau, 1st

The young designer trained under master Roger Vivier, but quickly made a name for himself with his outrageous concepts, including heels made of beer cans. He later popularized scarlet soles and heels of lucite with flowers or bits of fashionable rubbish trapped inside. Celebrities from Cher and Madonna to Princess Caroline of Monaco are fans. As is director David Lynch, who asked Louboutin to design shoes for an exposition at the Fondation Cartier (p. 25) in 2007. The shop is like a mini gallery, each shoe lovingly displayed against gilt foil or in a cubby-hole.

SEXY STILETTOS

46 **Rodolphe Menudier**

 14, rue de Castiglione, 1st

Space is at a premium in this luxury shopping parade near the place Vendôme, but designer Christophe Pillet has made a virtue of the intimacy with an interior that is as sleek and sexy as are Rodolphe Menudier's shoes. Having worked for Karl Lagerfeld, Paco Rabanne, Christian Lacroix and Chanel, Menudier certainly has the classic pedigree, but there is a rock 'n' roll edge to his stilettos, cork heels and fringes, not to mention his knee-high and over-the-knee boots, with such distinctive details as saucy straps and leather spaghetti laces.

It would be hard for anyone who appreciates colour and fabric to walk by Dominique Picquier's shop and not step inside. A textile designer with a penchant for plant life, Picquier specializes in monochrome canvas with abstract floral patterns printed in or reversed out of the background. 'I would like people to see my collection as a tribute to nature in the city,' she says. Bolts of fabrics as well as throws, bedspreads, cushion covers, curtains and an array of khaki-toned bags with heavy-duty stitched handles offer a unique blend of beauty and strength.

DOMINIQUE PICQUIER "F

78 **Jamin Puech**

24 68, rue Vieille-du-Temple, 3rd

14 **Peggy Huyn Kinh**

25 11, rue Coëtlogon, 6th

Benoît Jamin and Isabelle Puech's experimentation quickly brought them to the forefront of the fashion world: their first collection went on sale at Bergdorf Goodman and they have since created accessories for Chloé, Karl Lagerfeld and Balmain. Their original shop in the rue d'Hauteville is comfortable and welcoming, and is filled with their trademark leather pieces, all sporting the cheerful details for which the designers are known. Previously located in the area around the Canal St-Martin, the pair have since moved to the boutique-laden Marais.

As the bright-orange theme suggests, this shop is the headquarters of a bold designer who isn't afraid to stand out. Having worked as artistic director for Madame Grès, Balmain and Céline and as a scarf and leather designer for Cartier, Peggy Huyn Kinh ventured to produce her own label in 1996 and opened this shop in 2000. A heavy oak floor and leather-upholstered walls offset her creations, in crocodile, python and wild boar skin, which are striking even from the street. Rectilinear shapes frame her vibrant colours – orange, red and blue.

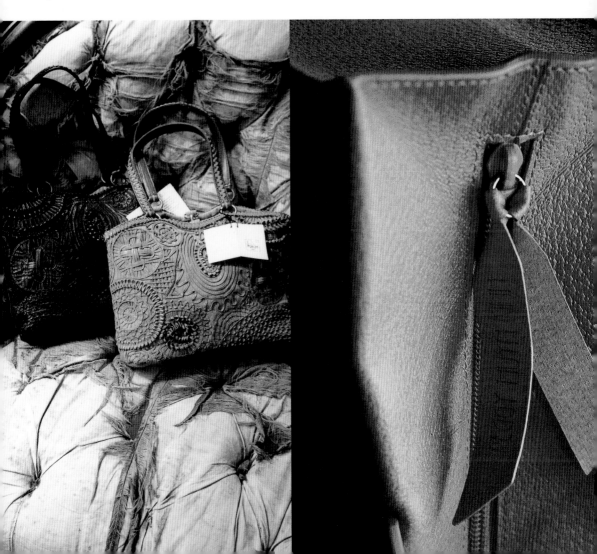

RELAXED CHIC

98 | **Isabel Marant**

18 | 16, rue de Charonne, 11th

Though her clothes are now sold in outlets around the world, Isabel Marant set up this first wood-filled boutique far from the fashion-following crowds of the Left Bank. Travels to Africa and India have influenced the clever draping that is her passion, but the young designer also has a whimsical side and a knack for surprising combinations. The shop is filled with such items as pretty, scoop-necked dresses and T-shirts that exhibit a taste for flounces, peasant-style tapestry skirts, ruffled skirts and tops in heavy crêpes, trouser suits in corduroy or hefty cotton velour, and heavy cotton jackets, all in complementary earth shades with the occasional gathered wrist or high neck. She has come a long way since this first shop opened, but she has stayed the course in a city known for its independent designers. Her version of boho-chic is still evolving and growing in popularity as her new shop on the rue de Seine in St-Germain-des-Prés and a concession in Printemps will attest. But this is still her home, and luckily for loyal clients she keeps it exciting with new collections and creative shop displays.

COOLEST CASHMERE
30 Lucien Pellat-Finet
8 1, rue de Montalembert, 7th

Christian Biecher, the designer's interior designer of the moment, has worked his bright magic to create an appropriately striking backdrop for Pellat-Finet's famed cashmere creations. A glass front marked by a pink awning and bright-red display shelves inside announce knitted wonders, T-shirts, pullovers and belted, tunic-length cardigans. The mere luxury of 100 per cent cashmere is not enough for the designer, who adds stripes, patterns and whimsical cut-out motifs to make eye-catching pieces that range from sporty to sophisticated.

PIÈCE UNIQUE
78 A-poc
22 47, rue des Francs-Bourgeois, 4th

'A-poc' stands for 'a piece of cloth' and is one of Issey Miyake's experiments in textile design. Like 'Pleats, Please', it takes a concept of fabric design – here, the cutting and assembling of one piece of cloth made from a single thread – and displays it in variation and as art. The concept has a showroom and workshop in the Marais by designers Ronan and Erwan Bouroullec (see also Galerie Kreo; p. 25), who've created white polystyrene circular display units to cradle coordinating sporty footwear and accessories. Some articles can be tailored to fit.

NEW COUTURE LINGERIE
30 Carine Gilson
5 18, rue de Grenelle, 7th

Competing in the Parisian lingerie market is a tough business, but designer Carine Gilson has taken on the challenge with a confident re-casting of lines, cuts and colours. The shop interior is all warm lighting with period details and a floral motif that constitute a real departure from the powder-puff presentation of older establishments. Her garments are designed in seasonal collections in styles and a colour palette that are a refreshing take on lingerie: not overly prim, nor shouting out for a centrefold, but dreamy, delicate and beautiful.

FEMININE FEELING

78 **Azzedine Alaïa**

8 7, rue de Moussy, 4th

Ring the bell on the blank façade and enter the world of Tunisian-born designer Azzedine Alaïa, whose lean, figure-hugging designs have won him a clientele of models and celebrities eager to show off their perfect forms in his designs. 'Sexy' doesn't begin to describe them – mannequins look as if they've been poured into tall, curvy moulds. They are made of delicately patterned knits, kid-like leather, crêpe or thick cotton weave. Next door is the most recent addition to the enclave of Alaïa, a retail temple to shoes designed by Marc Newson.

retreat

There is something for everyone wishing to escape the boulevards and the bustle of Paris. The cultural treasures and luscious landscape that have been the playgrounds of kings today offer a realm of gentility, rusticity, artistic inspiration and royal splendour. The getaways below offer four distinctly different experiences that are united by a love of the countryside and by the man-made riches that can be reaped from nature.

St-Germain-en-Laye: A Seat of Kings and a Modern Masterpiece

- Villa Savoye, Poissy
- Musée Claude Debussy, St-Germain-en-Laye
- La Forestière, St-Germain-en-Laye

Lying just at the outskirts of Paris's greater metropolitan area are two exquisite and wonderfully contrasting examples of modern design and genteel rusticity. At the end of a 40-minute suburban train ride, in Poissy, is one of the canonical and most famous residential buildings of the 20th century, designed by Le Corbusier. A few miles away lies the delightful town of St-Germain-en-Laye, the seat of royals before Versailles assumed the role. Designed by 1928, completed in 1931, saved from demolition in 1958 and restored in 1997, the Villa Savoye is the archetypal modern house – 'poetry produced by technology' – whose form and ideals have had an unparalleled influence on architects and designers around the world. Commissioned by Pierre Savoye for his wife and son on a site with views over the surrounding countryside, the house embodies Le Corbusier's development of domestic architecture as a 'machine for living'. With its main living quarters lifted up a level on stilts to provide the best views (and to allow for a 1927 Citroën to turn around), the house's 'cubistic' form is a complete history in modern architecture, a glimpse into the mind of a design visionary.

In sharp but pleasing contrast to the whiteness and pure form of Villa Savoye are the 17th-century stone mansions that give nearby St-Germain-en-Laye, birthplace of Louis XIV, its distinctly patrician air. Soaking up the atmosphere of the town might be enough for some, but for those wanting musical inspiration there is the Musée Claude Debussy, located in the house where the composer was born. For sweeping views over the Seine valley and gardens there is the château and its *terrasse*, designed by André Le Nôtre (see also p. 180). Towards the edge of town, on the rim of the St-Germain forest, lies an idyllic inn, La Forestière, set amid rose gardens and groves of trees and run since 1928 by generations of the Cazaudehore family, currently Philippe and his wife. While enjoying one of the suitably floral guest-rooms or inventive rustic-inspired dishes offered in the acclaimed restaurant, visitors can ponder the richness – and rich contrasts – of French architecture and countryside.

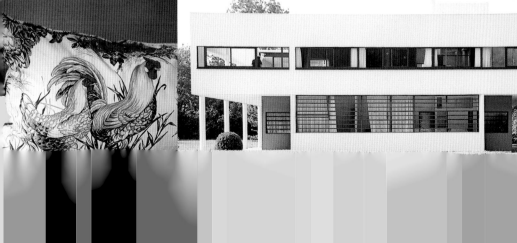

Barbizon: The Nature of Art and Landscape

- Musée Auberge du Père-Ganne, Barbizon
- Hôtellerie du Bas-Bréau, Barbizon
- Vaux le Vicomte, Maincy

Barbizon has been known as a 'painters' village' since the early 19th century, when a few artists settled here to take advantage of the inspiration of the enchanting Forest of Fontainebleau. Monet, Pissarro and Camille Corot are known to have painted here, Corot having 'discovered' Barbizon in the 1820s. By the mid-century, members of the Barbizon School, naturalist precursors to the Impressionists, had settled in, and the serene little village became a magnet for artists. Today, the tiny hamlet is full of galleries, artists' memorabilia and a number of aesthetically inclined visitors who come to enjoy the lush countryside or to wander down the art-filled rue Grande. The maison-atelier of Jean-François Millet, who became famous for his honest depictions of peasants in rural scenes, and that of Théodore Rousseau are open to the public, as is the Musée Auberge du Père-Ganne, a former inn whose walls and furniture are still marked by its artistic clientele.

With an afternoon's fill of the artist colony life, head happily inspired for the distinctly unpeasant-like comforts of the Hôtellerie du Bas-Bréau, a small luxury hotel with spacious rooms, a gourmet restaurant and outdoor swimming pool. You can enjoy a pre-dinner stroll through the park and gardens, perhaps a swim, and then settle in for an elegant meal prepared by staff who have entertained ambassadors and royalty. Some rooms include terraces overlooking the forest, a picturesque spot for the hotel's lavish breakfast of fresh fruits, pastries, ham, eggs, juice and coffee. All to keep you fortified for a hike into the 25,000 hectares of forest, where you might encounter the distinctly modern intervention of the *Cyclope*, a typically whimsical metal, mirror and hinged contraption designed by Jean Tinguely and his wife, Niki de St-Phalle.

You'll certainly want to save some time and energy for a trip to the grand château and gardens of Vaux le Vicomte, one of Europe's finest formal gardens and a short distance away. Built in 1661, with the finest and most extensive garden created by master landscape designer André Le Nôtre, it was also the inspiration for the envious Louis XIV to create his own grand dwelling – Versailles.

Reims: Champagne Civilization
• Château Les Crayères

Reims, an hour and a half by train from Gare de l'Est, is the capital of Champagne, a centre of Gothic splendour and host to one of the finest château-hotels in Europe, if not the world. From the soaring glories of the 13th-century cathedral, under whose vaults most of France's kings were crowned, to the subterranean treasures of the region's *grands marcs*, Reims provides a refined and sophisticated retreat for those in search of a dose of French history and its epicurean heights. Three of the city's architectural splendours (the cathedral, the 17th-century Tau palace and the Norman and Gothic St-Remi abbey and basilica) have been designated UNESCO World Heritage sites for their outstanding beauty. The cathedral's Gothic architecture and exceptional collection of stone statues are given a 20th-century twist in the form of stained-glass windows by Marc Chagall, and while the historic buildings might provide the focal points for a cultural visit, Reims is also dotted with numerous examples of Art Déco, the result of a massive post-war reconstruction in the 1920s involving more than 400 architects.

The elegant architecture provides the perfect backdrop to the culture of Champagne, which suffuses many aspects of the otherwise somewhat provincial town. While several of the the major Champagne houses offer free tours (G.H. Mumm & Cie, Pommery, Taittinger), a number require prior arrangement – an effort worth making to gain a more intimate understanding of the Champagne arts. Even better, try to arrange a trip into the countryside, where numerous smaller, often family-run producers provide a more personal look at the process, craft and love of making bubbly. Perhaps Reims's crowning achievement, the stylish blend of culture and gastronomic refinement, is Les Crayères, a distinguished *fin-de-siècle* château located a few minutes by taxi from the historic centre. Set in 7-hectare grounds, it is one of Europe's finest hotels, run by Elyane and Gérard Boyer, whose three Michelin-starred cuisine and nineteen-room accommodation attract a locally discerning clientele and international acclaim.

Le Château d'Esclimont: Palatial Escape

• La Rochefoucauld

Located between the magnet attractions of grandeur both secular and sacred, Versailles and Chartres, and only 45 minutes by train from central Paris, lies an outstanding French Renaissance château, surrounded by a moat and 60 hectares of parkland that offers fortunate visitors the chance to experience the atmosphere and drama of 16th-century French noble life – with all the modern conveniences. Begun in 1543, the château passed by sale and inheritance through generations of private ownership until it landed in the hands of the Rochefoucauld family, who finally sold it to the Grandes Étapes Françaises in 1981. It was turned into an appropriately grand forty-four-room hotel with decorative and artistic flourishes that preserve the character of a magnificent historic residence.

While some might find the presence of a swimming pool next to a rustic, centuries-old outbuilding disconcerting, others will appreciate the chance to enjoy a swim or a poolside cocktail with a view of the manicured formal gardens. The interiors are a delightful assemblage of period furnishings, wallcoverings, painted panellings, gilded woodwork and portraiture. Rooms are a riot of printed fabrics, with windows overlooking the vast arrangement of parterres, topiary and other plantings. A supremely romantic spot, especially in the evenings when the lit château glitters over the lake. The formal, 18th-century-style restaurant, La Rochefoucauld, is presided over by chef Olivier Dupart (formerly of Lucas-Carton, now Senderens; p. 140), whose modern menu pays homage to traditional cuisine and local produce. It's fine dining in an incomparable atmosphere. If you need an activity other than wafting about the rooms or exploring the gardens, golf and horse-riding are both on offer, or you can visit one of many nearby châteaux, or indeed the Gothic glories of magnificent Chartres, just over 16 kilometres away.

contact

All telephone numbers are given for dialling locally: the country code for France is 33; the city code for Paris is 01, which must be dialled before all eight-digit numbers. Calling from abroad, one dials (+33 1) plus the number given below. Telephone numbers in the retreat section are given for dialling from Paris: if calling from abroad, dial the country code (33) and drop the 0 in the number. The number in brackets by the name is the page number on which the entry appears.

0044 [82]
16, rue du Bourg-Tibourg
75004 Paris
T   42 76 00 44
E   info@0044paris.com
W   www.0044paris.com

15cent15 [151]
Hôtel Marignan
12, rue Marignan
75008 Paris
W   www.hotelmarignan.fr

3Rooms [130]
5, rue de Moussy
75004 Paris
T   44 78 92 00

A Priori Thé [54]
35–37, galerie Vivienne
75002 Paris
T   42 97 48 75

Alain Ducasse au Plaza Athénée [147]
Hôtel Plaza Athénée
25, avenue Montaigne
75008 Paris
T   53 67 65 00
E   adpa@alain-ducasse.com
W   www.alain-ducasse.com

Alexandre Biaggi [18]
14, rue de Seine
75006 Paris
T   44 07 34 73
E   info@alexandrebiaggi.com
W   www.alexandrebiaggi.com

Les Ambassadeurs [147]
Hôtel de Crillon
10, place de la Concorde
75008 Paris
T   44 71 16 16
E   ambassadeurs@crillon.com
W   www.crillon.com

L'Ambroisie [138]
9, place des Vosges
75004 Paris
T   42 78 51 45
E   ronan@ambroisie-placedesvosges.com
W   www.ambroisie-placedesvosges.com

L'Ami Jean [36]
27, rue Malar

75007 Paris
T   47 05 86 89

Anne Willi [106]
13, rue Keller
75011 Paris
T   48 06 74 06
E   info@annewilli.com
W   www.annewilli.com

Antoine et Lili [93]
95, quai de Valmy
75010 Paris
T   40 37 41 55
W   www.antoineetlili.com

L'Apparement Café [88]
18, rue des Coutures-St-Gervais
75003 Paris
T   48 87 12 22

A-poc [173]
47, rue des Francs-Bourgeois
75004 Paris
T   44 54 07 05
E   a-poc@issey-europe.com
W   www.isseymiyake.com

Archibooks [88]
18–20, rue de la Perle
75003 Paris
T   42 25 15 58
E   archibooks@archibooks.com
W   www.archibooks.com

Les Archives de la Presse [88]
51, rue des Archives
75003 Paris
T   42 72 63 93
E   info@lesarchivesdelapresse.com
W   www.lesarchivesdelapresse.com

Arnaud Delmontel [67]
39, rue des Martyrs
75009 Paris
T   48 78 29 33
E   contact@arnaud-delmontel.com
W   www.arnaud-delmontel.com

L'Arpège [144]
84, rue de Varenne
75007 Paris
T   47 05 09 06
E   arpege@alain-passard.com

W   www.alain-passard.com

Artazart [94]
83, quai de Valmy
75010 Paris
T   40 40 24 00
E   info@atrazart.com
W   www.artazart.com

Artcurial Café [40]
Hôtel Marcel Dassault
7, rond-point des Champs-Élysées
75008 Paris
T   42 99 16 16

As'Art [58]
3, passage du Grand-Cerf
75002 Paris
T   44 88 90 40
E   asart@wanadoo.fr
W   www.asart.fr

Association Createurs Goutte d'Or [73]
6, rue des Gardes
75018 Paris
T   41 50 38 67
E   sakina.msa@free.fr

Astier de la Villatte [49]
173, rue St-Honoré
75001 Paris
T   42 60 74 13
W   www.astierdevillatte.com

L'Astrance [138]
4, rue Beethoven
75016 Paris
T   40 50 84 40

L'Atmosphère [94]
49, rue Lucien-Sampaix
75010 Paris
T   40 38 09 21

Au Bourguignon du Marais [85]
52, rue François-Miron
75004 Paris
T   48 87 15 40

L'Avant-Goût [26]
26, rue Bobillot
75013 Paris
T   53 80 24 00

Azzedine Alaïa [175]
7, rue de Moussy

75004 Paris
T   42 72 19 19

Les Bains du Marais [82]
31–33, rue des Blancs-Manteaux
75004 Paris
T   44 61 02 02
E   contact@lesbainsdumarais.com
W   www.lesbainsdumarais.com

Balouga [90]
25, rue des Filles du Calvaire
75003 Paris
T   42 74 01 49
E   info@balouga.com
W   www.balouga.com

Bar du Plaza Athénée [155]
Hôtel Plaza Athénée
25, avenue Montaigne
75008 Paris
T   53 67 66 65
W   www.plaza-athenee-paris.com

Le Baratin [153]
3, rue Jouye-Rouve
75020 Paris
T   43 49 39 70

be boulangépicier [40]
73, boulevard de Courcelles
75008 Paris
T   46 22 20 20
E   boulangepicier@wanadoo.fr
W   www.boulangepicier.com

La Belle Hortense [87]
31, rue Vieille-du-Temple
75004 Paris
T   48 04 71 60
E   info@cafeine.com
W   www.cafeine.com

Belle de Jour [73]
7, rue Tardieu
75018 Paris
T   46 06 15 28

Le Bellechasse [114]
8, rue de Bellechasse
75007 Paris
T   45 50 22 31
E   info@lebellechasse.com
W   www.lebellechasse.com

Benoît [81]
20, rue St-Martin

75004 Paris
T 42 72 25 76
E restaurant.benoit@wanadoo.fr
W www.alain-ducasse.com

Bercy Village [100]
28, rue François Truffaut
75012 Paris
T 40 02 90 80
E presse@bercyvillage.com
W www.bercyvillage.com

Berthillon [85]
31, rue St-Louis-en-l'Île
75004 Paris
T 43 54 31 61

Bistrot Paul Bert [104]
18, rue Paul-Bert
75011 Paris
T 43 72 24 01

Blancs Manteaux [82]
42, rue des Blancs-Manteaux
75004 Paris
T 42 71 70 00
E postmaster@
   blancsmanteaux.com
W www.blancsmanteaux.com

Le Bon Marché [163]
24, rue de Sèvres
75007 Paris
T 44 39 80 00
W www.lebonmarche.fr

La Boutique de la CSAO [86]
9, rue Elzévir
75003 Paris
T 42 71 33 17
W www.csao.fr

**Brasserie de
l'Île St-Louis** [85]
55, quai de Bourbon
75004 Paris
T 43-54-02-59

Brasserie Printemps [64]
Printemps de la Mode, 6th floor
64, boulevard Haussmann
75009 Paris
T 42.82.49.03
W http://departmentstoreparis.
   printemps

Breizh Café [87]
109, rue Vieille-du-Temple
75003 Paris
T 42 72 13 77
W www.breizhcafe.com

By Terry [55]
36, galerie Véro-Dodat
75001 Paris
T 44 76 00 76

Café A [94]
Maison d'Architecture
148, rue du Faubourg St-Martin
75010 Paris
T 40 34 06 57
E contact@maisonarchitecture-

idf.org
W www.maisonarchitecture-
   idf.org

Café Constant [36]
139, rue St-Dominique
75007 Paris
T 47 53 75 34
E web@leviolonlondingres.com
W www.leviolonlondingres.com

Café de l'Industrie [109]
16, rue St-Sabin
75011 Paris
T 47 00 13 53

Le Café Marly [49]
Palais du Louvre
93, rue de Rivoli
75001 Paris
T 49 26 06 60

**Café de la Nouvelle
Mairie** [17]
19–21, rue des Fossés-St-Jacques
75005 Paris
T 44 07 04 41

Café du Passage [106]
12, rue de Charonne
75011 Paris
T 49 29 97 64

Café du Trésor [87]
7–9, rue du Trésor
75004 Paris
T 42 71 32 91

Les Cailloux [26]
58, rue des Cinq-Diamants
75013 Paris
T 45 80 15 08

Le Caméléon [25]
6, rue de Chevreuse
75006 Paris
T 43 27 43 27

Canzi [85]
4, rue Ferdinand Duval
75004 Paris
T 42 78 09 37
E canzi@canzi.fr
W www.canzi.fr

Carine Gilson [174]
18, rue de Grenelle
75007 Paris
T 43 26 46 71
E info@carinegilson.com
W www.carinegilson.com

Carré Rive Gauche [35]
75007 Paris
E crg@carrerivegauche.com
W www.carrerivegauche.com

Caves Miard [153]
9, rue des Quatre-Vents
75006 Paris
T 43 54 99 30

Les Caves Pétrissans [40]
30 bis, avenue Niel
75017 Paris
T 42 27 52 03

Centre Pompidou [80]
place Georges Pompidou
75004 Paris
T 44 78 12 33
W www.centrepompidou.fr

Chai 33 [100]
Bercy Village
33, cour St-Émilion
75012 Paris
T 53 44 01 01
E info@chai33.com
W www.chai33.com

Les Charpentiers [20]
10, rue Mabillon
75006 Paris
T 43 26 30 05

Charvet [49]
28, place Vendôme
75001 Paris
T 42 60 30 70

Le Chateaubriand [145]
129, avenue Parmentier
75011 Paris
T 43 57 45 95

Chéri Bibi [74]
15, rue André del Sarte
75018 Paris
T 42.54.88.96

Chez Camille [71]
8, rue Ravignan
75018 Paris
T 46 06 05 78

Chez Georges [135]
1, rue du Mail
75002 Paris
T 42 60 07 11

Chez Jean [67]
8, rue St-Lazare
75009 Paris
T 48 78 62 73

Chez Michel [94]
10, rue de Belzunce
75010 Paris
T 44 53 06 20

Chez les 'On' [109]
49, rue de la Chine
75020 Paris
T 44 62 93 31

Chez Paul [26]
22, rue de la Butte-aux-Cailles
75013 Paris
T 45 89 22 11

Chez Prune [93]
71, quai de Valmy
75010 Paris
T 42 41 30 47

Le Chiberta [40]
3, rue Arsène-Houssaye
75008 Paris
T 53 53 42 00
E chiberta@guysavoy.com
W www.lechiberta.com

**Christian
Astuguevieille** [54]
42, galerie Vivienne
75002 Paris
T 42 60 10 70

Christian Louboutin [169]
19, rue Jean-Jacques-Rousseau
75001 Paris
T 42 36 05 31
E soudabe@christianlouboutin.fr
W www.christianlouboutin.com

Le Cinquante [93]
50, rue de Lancry
75010 Paris
T 42 02 36 83

**La Cité de l'Architecture et
du Patrimoine** [39]
1, place du Trocadéro et du 11
   Novembre
75116 Paris
T 58 51 52 00
W www.citechaillot.fr

Claude Jeantet [54]
10, rue Thérèse
75001 Paris
T 42 86 01 36

La Cloche des Halles [57]
28, rue Coquillière
75001 Paris
T 42 36 93 89

CMO [51]
5, rue Chabanais
75002 Paris
T 40 20 45 98

Colette [50]
213, rue St-Honoré
75001 Paris
T 55 35 33 90
E contact@colette.fr
W www.colette.fr

Collection [88]
4, rue de Thorigny
75003 Paris
T 42 78 67 74
E collection@ateliersdart.com
W www.ateliersdart.com

The Collection [90]
33, rue de Poitou
75003 Paris
T 42 77 04 20

**Comme des Garçons
Parfums** [165]
23, place du Marché-St-Honoré
75001 Paris
T 47 03 15 03

Comptoir de l'Image [85]
44, rue de Sévigné
75003 Paris
T 42 72 03 92

La Corbeille [58]
5, passage du Grand-Cerf
75002 Paris
T 53 40 78 77
E lacorbeille@wanadoo.fr
W www.lacorbeille.fr

Coude Fou [82]
12, rue du Bourg-Tibourg
75004 Paris
T 42 77 15 16
W www.lecoudefou.com

Couleurs Canal [93]
56, rue de Lancry
75010 Paris
T 42 40 60 52

Courrèges [43]
40, rue François-1er
75008 Paris
T 53 67 30 00
E courreges@courreges.com
W www.courreges.com

Créations Cherif [103]
13, avenue Daumesnil
75012 Paris
T 43 40 01 00
E info@creations-cherif.com
W www.creations-cherif.com

The Cristal Room [146]
11, place des États-Unis
75016 Paris
T 40 22 11 10
E cristalroom@baccarat.fr
W www.baccarat.fr

Da Rosa [18]
62, rue de Seine
75006 Paris
T 40 51 00 09

De la Ville Café [159]
34, boulevard Bonne-Nouvelle
75010 Paris
T 48 24 48 09

Declercq Passementiers [58]
15, rue Étienne-Marcel
75001 Paris
T 44 76 90 70
E declercq@
declercqpassementiers.fr
W www.declercqpassementiers.fr

Delicabar [33]
Le Bon Marché, 1st floor
26–38, rue de Sèvres
75007 Paris
T 42 22 10 12
E hsamuel@delicabar.fr
W www.delicabar.fr

Delphine Charlotte-Parmentier [82]
26, rue du Bourg-Tibourg
75004 Paris
T 44 54 51 73
E contact@dcp-corp.com
W www.dcp-corp.com

Detaille [67]
10, rue St-Lazare
75009 Paris
T 48 78 68 50
W www.detaille.com

Deuce [58]
7, rue d'Aboukir
75002 Paris
T 42 21 12 95
E info@deuce.fr
W www.deuce.fr

Didier Ludot [52]
Vintage: 20–24, galerie de
    Montpensier
75001 Paris
T 42 96 06 56
La Petite Robe Noire: 125, galerie
    de Valois
75001 Paris
T 40 15 01 04
E wallis@didierludot.com
W www.didierludot.com

Le Dokhan's [156]
Hôtel Sofitel
117, rue Lauriston
75116 Paris
T 53 65 66 99
E reservation@dokhans.com
W www.sofitel.com

Le Dôme Montparnasse [23]
108, boulevard du Montparnasse
75014 Paris
T 42 63 48 18

Dominique Picquier [170]
10, rue Charlot
75003 Paris
T 42 72 23 32
E boutique@
dominiquepicquier.com
W www.dominiquepicquier.com

Le Doudingue [71]
24, rue Durantin
75018 Paris
T 42 54 88 08

Drouant [51]
16–18, place Gaillon
75002 Paris
T 42 65 15 16
E reservations@drouant.com
W www.drouant.com

L'Ebauchoir [104]
43–45, rue de Cîteaux
75012 Paris
T 43 42 49 31
W www.lebauchoir.com

L'Ecailler du Bistrot [104]
22, rue Paul-Bert
75011 Paris
T 43 72 76 77

Editions de Parfums Frédéric Malle [165]
37, rue de Grenelle
75007 Paris
T 42 22 76 40
E contact@
editionsdeparfums.com
W www.editionsdeparfums.com

Église du Dôme [36]
Hôtel des Invalides
129, rue de Grenelle
75007 Paris
T 44 42 37 72
E accueil-ma@invalides.org
W www.invalides.org

Église St-Jean de Montmartre [71]
19, rue des Abbesses
75018 Paris
T 46 06 43 96
W www.
    saintjeandemontmartre.com

Église St-Louis-en-l'Île [85]
19 bis, rue St-Louis-en-l'Île
75004 Paris
T 46 34 11 60
E saintlouis.enlile@free.fr

Emmanuelle Zysman [67]
81, rue des Martyrs
75018 Paris
T 42 52 01 00

L'Entracte [72]
44, rue d'Orsel
75018 Paris
T 46 06 93 41

L'Épi Dupin [33]
11, rue Dupin
75006 Paris
T 42 22 64 56
E contact@epidupin.com
W www.epidupin.com

Et dans mon coeur il y a [93]
56, rue de Lancry
75010 Paris
T 42 38 07 37

Et puis c'est tout [68]
72, rue des Martyrs
75018 Paris
T 40 23 94 02

L'Étoile Manquante [87]
34, rue Vielle-du-Temple
75004 Paris
T 42 72 48 34
W www.cafeine.com

Les Fables de la Fontaine [36]
131, rue St-Dominique
75007 Paris

T 44 18 37 55
E web@leviolondingres.com
W www.leviolondingres.com

Fanche et Flo [71]
19, rue Durantin
75018 Paris
T 42 51 24 18

Les Fines Gueules [55]
2, rue de la Vrillière
75001 Paris
T 42 61 35 41

Fish/La Boissonerie [20]
69, rue de Seine
75006 Paris
T 43 54 34 69

Florence Loewy [88]
9–11, rue de Thorigny
75003 Paris
T 44 78 98 45
E flo@florenceloewy.com
W www.florenceloewy.com

Fondation Cartier [25]
261, boulevard Raspail
75014 Paris
T 42 18 56 51
W www.fondation.cartier.fr

Fondation Le Corbusier [39]
8–10, square du Docteur-Blanche
75016 Paris
T 42 88 41 53
E info@fondationlecorbusier.fr
W www.fondationlecorbusier.fr

Fondation Dina Vierny – Musée Maillol [35]
59–61, rue de Grenelle
75007 Paris
T 42 22 59 58
E contact@museemaillol.com
W www.museemaillol.com

Fondation Pierre Bergé, Yves St Laurent [40]
5, avenue Marceau
75116 Paris
T 44 31 64 00
W www.fondation-pb-ysl.net

La Fourmi Café [69]
74, rue des Martyrs
75018 Paris
T 42.64.70.35

FR66 [81]
25, rue du Renard
75004 Paris
T 44 54 35 36
E info@fr66.com
W www.fr66.com

Le Fumoir [159]
6, rue de l'Amiral-de-Coligny
75001 Paris
T 42 92 00 24
W www.lefumoir.fr

FuturWare Lab [69]
2, rue Piémontési
75018 Paris
T   42 23 66 08
E   ltania@magic.fr
W   http://membres.lycos.fr/
    futurwarelab

Gaëlle Barré [106]
17, rue Keller
75011 Paris
T   43 14 63 02
E   commercial@gaellebarre.com
W   www.gaellebarre.com

La Galerie 3A [86]
9, rue Elzévir
75003 Paris
W   www.csao.fr

Galerie 54 [22]
54, rue Mazarine
75006 Paris
T   43 26 89 96
E   galerie54@club-internet.fr
W   www.galerie54.com

**La Galerie
d'Architecture** [86]
11, rue des Blancs-Manteaux
75004 Paris
T   49 96 64 00
E   mail@galerie-architecture.fr
W   www.galerie-architecture.fr

Galerie Chez Valentin [85]
9, rue St-Gilles
75003 Paris
T   48 87 42 55
E   galerie@
    galeriechezvalentin.com
W   www.galeriechezvalentin.com

**Galerie Christine
Diegoni** [72]
47 ter, rue d'Orsel
75018 Paris
T   42 64 69 48
E   christinediegoni@wanadoo.fr
W   www.christinediegoni.fr

Galerie Doria [18]
16, rue de Seine
75006 Paris
T   43 25 43 25
E   galerie.doria@wanadoo.fr

Galerie Hélène Porée [20]
1, rue de l'Odéon
75006 Paris
T   43 54 17 00
E   info@galerie-helene-
    poree.com
W   www.galerie-helene-
    poree.com

Galerie de l'Instant [90]
46, rue de Poitou
75003 Paris
T   44 54 94 09

Galerie Kreo [25]
11, rue Louise-Weiss

75013 Paris
E   kreogal@wanadoo.fr
W   www.galeriekreo.com

Galerie du Passage [55]
20–26, galerie Véro-Dodat
75001 Paris
T   42 36 01 13
E   contact@
    galeriedupassage.com
W   www.galeriedupassage.com

Galerie Patrick Fourtin [57]
9, rue des Bons-Enfants
75001 Paris
T   42 60 12 63

Galerie Patrick Seguin [106]
5, rue des Taillandiers
75011 Paris
T   47 00 32 35
E   info@patrickseguin.com
W   www.patrickseguin.com

Galerie Praz-Delavallade
[25]
28, rue Louise-Weiss
75013 Paris
T   45 86 20 00
E   gallery@praz-delavallade.com
W   www.praz-delavallade.com

Galerie Vivienne [54]
entrances at 4, rue des Petits-
Champs and 6, rue Vivienne
75002 Paris
E   contact@galerie-vivienne.com
W   www.galerie-vivienne.com

Gallopin [137]
40, rue Notre-Dame-des-Victoires
75002 Paris
T   42 36 45 38
E   administration@
    brasseriegallopin.com
W   www.brasseriegallopin.com

Gaspard de la Butte [71]
10 bis, rue Yvonne-le-Tac
75018 Paris
T   42 55 99 40
E   contact@
    gasparddelabutte.com
W   www.gasparddelabutte.com

Gaya Rive Gauche [35]
44, rue du Bac
75007 Paris
T   45 44 73 73
E   info@pierregagnaire.com
W   www.pierre-gagnaire.com

La Gazzetta [139]
29, rue de Cotte
75012 Paris
T   43 47 47 05
E   info@lagazzetta.fr
W   www.lagazzetta.fr

Georges [80]
Centre Pompidou, 6th Floor
place Georges Pompidou
75004 Paris

T   44 78 47 99

Le Grand Véfour [137]
17, rue de Beaujolais
75001 Paris
T   42 96 56 27
E   contact@legrandvefour.fr
W   www.grand-vefour.com

**La Grande Boutique de
l'Artisan Parfumeur** [57]
2, rue l'Amiral-de-Coligny
75001 Paris
T   44 88 27 50
W   www.laboutiquedelartisan
    parfumeur.com

Guerlain [166]
68, avenue des Champs-Élysées
75008 Paris
T   45 62 11 21
E   irousseau@guerlain.fr
W   www.guerlain.com

Guy Savoy [134]
18, rue Troyon
75017 Paris
T   43 80 40 61
E   reserv@guysavoy.com
W   www.guysavoy.com

L'Habilleur [90]
44, rue de Poitou
75003 Paris
T   48 87 77 12

Heaven [67]
83, rue des Martyrs
75018 Paris
T   44 92 92 92
E   informations@heaven-
    paris.com
W   www.heaven-paris.com

L'Hôtel [128]
13, rue des Beaux-Arts
75006 Paris
T   44 41 99 00
E   stay@l-hotel.com
W   www.l-hotel.com

Hôtel Amour [122]
8, rue Navarin
75009 Paris
T   48 78 31 80
E   hotelamour@hotmail.fr
W   www.hotelamour.com

Hôtel Bourg Tibourg [120]
19, rue du Bourg-Tibourg
75004 Paris
T   42 78 47 39
E   hotel@bourgtibourg.com
W   www.hotelbourgtibourg.com

Hôtel Costes [158]
239, rue St-Honoré
75001 Paris
T   42 44 50 00
W   www.hotelcostes.com

Hôtel Daniel [126]
8, rue Frédéric Bastiat

75008 Paris
T   42 56 17 00
E   hoteldanielparis@
    hoteldanielparis.com
W   www.hoteldanielparis.com

L'Hôtel du Nord [94]
102, quai de Jemmapes
75010 Paris
T   40 40 78 78
W   www.hoteldunord.org

**L'Hôtel Particulier de
Montmartre** [118]
23, avenue Junot
75018 Paris
T   53 41 81 40
E   hotelparticulier@orange.fr
W   www.hotel-particulier-
    montmartre.com

L'Hôtel de Sers [116]
41, avenue Pierre 1er de Serbie
75008 Paris
T   53 23 75 75
E   resa@hoteldesers.com
W   www.hoteldesers.com

La Hune [22]
170, boulevard St-Germain
75006 Paris
T   45 48 35 85

Institut du Monde Arabe [17]
1, rue des Fossés-St-Bernard
75005 Paris
T   40 51 38 38
E   rap@imarabe.org
W   www.imarabe.org

Isabel Marant [172]
16, rue de Charonne
75011 Paris
T   49 29 71 55
E   n.chemouny@
    isabelmarant.tm.fr
W   www.isabelmarant.tm.fr

Jamin Puech [171]
68, rue Vieille-du-Temple
75003 Paris
T   48 87 84 87
E   cial@jamin-puech.com
W   www.jamin-puech.com

JAR [164]
14, rue de Castiglione
75001 Paris
T   40 20 47 20
E   capitals@jar-parfums.fr
W   www.jar-parfums.fr

Jean Paul Gaultier [42]
44, avenue George V
75008 Paris
T   44 43 00 44
W   www.jeanpaulgaultier.com

Jean Paul Gaultier [54]
6, galerie Vivienne
75002 Paris
T   42 86 05 05
W   www.jeanpaulgaultier.com

Jérémie Barthod [72]
7, rue des Trois Frères
70018 Paris
T 42 62 54 50
E jeremiebarthod@free.fr
W www.jeremiebarthod.com

Le Jokko [86]
5, rue Elzévir
75003 Paris
T 42 74 35 96
W www.csao.fr

Juvenile's [50]
47, rue de Richelieu
75001 Paris
T 42 97 46 49

Karine Arabian [64]
4, rue Papillon
75009 Paris
T 45 23 23 24
E info@karinearabian.com
W www.karinearabian.com

Ken Okada [35]
1 bis, rue de la Chaise
75007 Paris
T 42 55 18 81
E contact@ken-okada.com
W www.ken-okada.com

Kiliwatch [58]
64, rue Tiquetonne
75002 Paris
T 42 21 17 37
W www.kiliwatch.fr

Legrand Filles et Fils [152]
1, rue de la Banque
75002 Paris
T 42 60 07 12
E info@caves-legrand.com
W www.caves-legrand.com

Librairie Gourmande [58]
90, rue Montmartre
75002 Paris
T 43 54 37 27
W www.librairie-gourmande.fr

Librairie le Moniteur [20]
7, place de l'Odéon
75006 Paris
T 44 41 15 75
W www.groupemoniteur.fr

Lieu Commun [90]
5, rue des Filles du Calvaire
75003 Paris
T 44 54 08 30
E info@lieucommun.fr
W www.lieucommun.fr

Lily Latifi [74]
11, rue des Gardes
75018 Paris
T 42 23 30 86
E lily@lilylatifi.com
W www.lilylatifi.com

Louise 13 [25]
rue Louise-Weiss
75013 Paris
T 48 51 33 21
E louise13@freesurf.fr
W www.louise13.fr

Le Louvre des Antiquaires [57]
2, place du Palais-Royal
75001 Paris
T 42 97 27 00
W www.louvre-antiquaires.com

Luc Dognin [73]
4, rue des Gardes
75018 Paris
T 44 92 32 16
E dognin@dogninparis.com
W www.dogninparis.com

Lucien Pellat-Finet [173]
1, rue de Montalembert
75007 Paris
T 42 22 22 77
E parisboutique@
lucienpellat-finet.com
W www.lucienpellat-finet.com

Les Lunetiers Delambre [90]
10, rue des Filles du Calvaire
75003 Paris
T 43 21 71 00
E contact@lunetiers-
delambre.com
W http://
lunetiersdelambre.free.fr

La Maison de l'Aubrac [43]
37, rue Marbeuf
75008 Paris
T 43 59 05 14
W www.maison-aubrac.com

Maison Calavas [167]
13, rue Royale, 2nd floor
75008 Paris
T 40 07 57 57
W www.maisoncalavas-
boutique.com

Maison Fey [103]
15, avenue Daumesnil
75012 Paris
T 43 41 22 22
E contact@maisonfey.com
W www.maisonfey.com

La Maison Rouge, Fondation Antoine de Galbert [103]
10, boulevard de la Bastille
75012 Paris
T 40 01 08 81
E info@lamaisonrouge.org
W www.lamaisonrouge.org

La Maison des Trois Thés [154]
33, rue Gracieuse
75005 Paris
T 43 36 93 84

Malhia [103]
19, avenue Daumesnil

75012 Paris
T 53 44 76 76

Le Marché d'Aligre [104]
place d'Aligre
75012 Paris
W http://marchedaligre.free.fr

Márcia de Carvalho [73]
2, rue des Gardes
75018 Paris
T 42 51 64 05
E marciadecarvalho@free.fr
W www.marciadecarvalho.com

Mariage Frères [82]
35, rue du Bourg-Tibourg
75004 Paris
T 43 47 18 54
E info@mariagefreres.com
W www.mariagefreres.com

Marie Lavande [103]
83, avenue Daumesnil
75012 Paris
T 44 67 78 78
W www.marie-lavande.com

La Marine [93]
55 bis, quai de Valmy
75010 Paris
T 42 39 69 81

Martin Grant [88]
10, rue Charlot
75003 Paris
T 42 71 39 49
E contact@
martingrantparis.com
W www.martingrantparis.com

Martin Margiela [52]
25 bis, rue de Montpensier
75001 Paris
T 40 15 07 55
E 25montpensier_paris@
martinmargiela.net
W www.martinmargiela.com

La Mère de Famille [64]
35, rue du Faubourg-Montmartre
75009 Paris
T 47 70 83 69
E contact@lameredefamille.com
W www.lameredefamille.com

La Mère Lachaise [109]
78, boulevard de Ménilmontant
75020 Paris
T 47 97 61 60

Mira Belle [72]
6, place Charles-Dullin
75018 Paris
T 42 52 00 11
E mira-belle-chapeaux@
hotmail.fr
W www.mira-belle.fr

MK2 Bibliothèque [26]
128–162, avenue de France
75013 Paris
T 08 92 68 14 07

W www.mk2.com

Mon Vieil Ami [85]
69, rue St-Louis-en- l'Île
75004 Paris
T 40 46 01 35
W www.mon-vieil-ami.com

Moon Young Hee [93]
62, rue Charlot
75003 Paris
T 42 72 12 59

La Mosquée de Paris [150]
39, rue Geoffroy-St-Hilaire
75005 Paris
T 43 31 38 20
E contact@
lamosqueedeparis.com
W www.la-mosquee.com

Murano Urban Resort [124]
13, boulevard du Temple
75003 Paris
T 42 71 20 00
E paris@muranoresort.com
W www.muranoresort.com

Murano Urban Resort Bar [158]
Murano Urban Resort
13, boulevard du Temple
75003 Paris
T 42 71 20 00
W www.muranoresort.com

La Muse Vin [109]
101, rue de Charonne
75011 Paris
T 40 09 93 05

Musée des Arts Décoratifs [49]
107, rue de Rivoli
75001 Paris
T 44 55 57 50
W www.lesartsdecoratifs.fr

Musée Bourdelle [36]
18, rue Antoine Bourdelle
75015 Paris
T 49 54 73 73
W www.bourdelle.paris.fr

Le Musée Cognacq-Jay [86]
8, rue Elzévir
75003 Paris
T 40 27 07 21

Musée Gustave Moreau [67]
14, rue de La Rochefoucauld
75009 Paris
T 48 74 38 50
E info@musee-moreau.fr
W www.musee-moreau.fr

Musée Jacquemart André [64]
158, boulevard Haussmann
75008 Paris
T 45 62 11 59
E message@musee-
jacquemart-andre.com

W www.musee-jacquemart-
andre.com

**Musée Nissim de
Camondo** [64]
63, rue de Monceau
75008 Paris
T 53 89 06 40
W www.ucad.fr

Musée de l'Orangerie [49]
Jardin des Tuileries
75001 Paris
T 44 77 80 07
E information-orangerie@
culture.gouv.fr
W www.musee-orangerie.fr

Musée du Quai Branly [36]
37, quai Branly
75007 Paris
T 56 61 70 00
W www.quaibranly.fr

**Musée de la Vie
Romantique** [68]
Hôtel Scheffer-Renan
16, rue Chaptal
75009 Paris
T 48 74 95 38

Muskhane [90]
3, rue Pastourelle
75003 Paris
T 42 71 07 00
E contact@muskhane.com
W www.muskhane.com

Onze [109]
11, rue Oberkampf
75011 Paris
T 43 55 32 11
W www.onzedesign.com

Pages 50/70 [71]
15, rue Yvonne-le-Tac
75018 Paris
T 42 52 48 59
E olivier.verlet@wanadoo.fr
W www.pages50-70.com

La Pagode [33]
57 bis, rue de Babylone
75007 Paris
T 45 55 48 48

Pain de Sucres [82]
14, rue Rambuteau
75003 Paris
T 45 74 68 92

Palais de Tokyo [39]
13, avenue du Président-Wilson
75016 Paris
T 47 23 54 01
E info@palaisdetokyo.com
W www.palaisdetokyo.com

La Palette [23]
43, rue de Seine
75006 Paris
T 43 26 68 15

Pamp'lune [69]
4 bis, rue Piémontési
75018 Paris
T 46 06 50 23
W http://pamp-lune.com

Les Papilles [17]
30, rue Gay-Lussac
75005 Paris
T 43 25 20 79

Parc André Citroën [39]
quai André-Citroën
75015 Paris

Parc de Bercy [100]
quai de Bercy
75012 Paris

Passage de Retz [93]
9, rue Charlot
75003 Paris
T 48 04 37 99
E welcome@passagederetz.com
W www.passagederetz.com

Patricia Louisor [69]
16, rue Houdon
75018 Paris
T 42 62 10 42
E info@patricialouisor.com
W www.patricialouisor.com

**Pavillon de
l'Arsenal** [103]
21, boulevard Morland
75004 Paris
T 42 76 33 97
E infopa@pavillon-arsenal.com
W www.pavillon-arsenal.com

Peggy Huyn Kinh [171]
11, rue Coëtlogon
75006 Paris
T 42 84 83 83

Le Petit Dakar [86]
6, rue Elzévir
75003 Paris
T 44 59 34 74
W www.csao.fr

Le Petit Pontoise [17]
9, rue de Pontoise
75005 Paris
T 43 29 25 20

Pierre Gagnaire [142]
Hôtel Balzac
6, rue Balzac
75008 Paris
T 58 36 12 50
E info@pierregagnaire.com
W www.pierre-gagnaire.com

Pierre Hardy [168]
Jardins du Palais Royal
156, galerie de Valois
75001 Paris
T 42 60 59 75
E boutique@pierrehardy.com
W www.pierrehardy.com

Pierre Hermé [164]
72, rue Bonaparte
75006 Paris
T 43 54 47 77
E info@pierreherme.com
W www.pierreherme.com

Le Pré Catalan [141]
route de Suresnes
Bois de Boulogne
75016 Paris
T 44 14 41 14
W www.precatelanparis.com

Le Pré Verre [18]
8, rue Thénard
75005 Paris
T 43 54 59 47
W www.lepreverre.com

Publicis Drugstore [42]
133, avenue des Champs-Élysées
75008 Paris
T 44 43 79 00
E contact@
publicisdrugstore.com
W www.publicisdrugstore.com

Rautureau [82]
16, rue du Bourg-Tibourg
75004 Paris
T 42 77 01 55

Le Réfectoire [106]
80, boulevard Richard Lenoir
75011 Paris
T 48 06 74 85
W http://lerefectoire.free.fr

La Régalade [143]
49, avenue Jean-Moulin
75014 Paris
T 45 45 68 58
E la_regalade@yahoo.fr

Résonances [100]
Bercy Village
9–11, cour St-Émilion
75012 Paris
T 44 73 82 82
E bercy.village@resonances.fr
W www.resonances.fr

Ribouldingue [18]
10, rue St-Julien-le-Pauvre
75005 Paris
T 46 33 98 80

Rodolphe Menudier [169]
14, rue de Castiglione
75001 Paris
T 42 60 86 27
E rodolphe@
rodolphemenudier.com
W www.rodolphemenudier.com

Roger Lanne [103]
103, avenue Daumesnil
75012 Paris
T 43 40 67 67
E roger.lanne@free.fr
W http://roger.lanne.free.fr

Rose Bakery [67]
46, rue des Martyrs
75009 Paris
T 42 82 12 80

Rosebud [25]
11 bis, rue Delambre
75014 Paris
T 43 35 38 54

Sadaharu Aoki [25]
56, boulevard de Port Royal
75005 Paris
T 45 35 36 80
E paris@sadaharuaoki.com
W www.sadaharuaoki.com

Sandrine Philippe [57]
6, rue Hérold
75001 Paris
T 40 26 21 78
E sandrinephilippepress@
gmail.com

Le Saut du Loup [150]
107, rue de Rivoli
75001 Paris
T 42 25 49 55
W www.lesautduloup.com

Senderens [140]
9, place de la Madeleine
75008 Paris
T 42 65 22 90
E restaurant@senderens.fr
W www.senderens.fr

Sennelier [35]
3, quai Voltaire
75007 Paris
T 42 60 72 15
E magasinsennelier@wanadoo.fr
W www.magasinsennelier.com

Senteurs de Fée [72]
47 bis, rue d'Orsel
75018 Paris
T 42 52 25 98

Sentou Galerie [163]
24, rue du Pont Louis-Philippe
75004 Paris
T 42 77 44 79
E sentou.marais@sentou.fr
W www.sentou.fr

Serge Amoruso [104]
13, rue Abel
75012 Paris
T 43 45 14 10
E contact@sergeamoruso.com
W www.sergeamoruso.com

Le Soleil [74]
109, avenue Michelet
75018 Paris
T 40 10 08 08
E lesoleil2@orange.fr
W www.restaurantlesoleil.com

Le Souk [106]
1, rue Keller
75011 Paris

T 49 29 05 08
W www.lesoukfr.com

Sous les Joups [157]
12, rue Durantin
75018 Paris
T 42 52 51 40
W www.souslesjupes.eu

Spa Nuxe [58]
32, rue Montorgueil
75001 Paris
T 55 80 71 40
E le32montorgueil@nuxe.com
W www.nuxe.com

Spring [67]
28, rue de la Tour d'Auvergne
75009 Paris
T 45 96 05 72
E freshsnail@free.fr
W http://
  springparis.blogspot.com

Le Square Trousseau [104]
1, rue Antoine-Vollon
75012 Paris
T 43 43 06 00

Stella Cadente [94]
93, quai de Valmy
75010 Paris
T 42 09 27 00
E contact@
  stellacadenteparfums.net
W www.stella-cadente.com

Suave [26]
20, rue de la Providence
75013 Paris
T 45 89 99 27

Surface to Air [57]
46, rue l'Arbre-Sec
75001 Paris
T 49 27 04 58
W www.surface2air.com

Suzanne Tarasiève [25]
171, rue du Chevaleret
75013 Paris
T 45 86 02 02
E info@suzanne-tarasieve.com
W www.suzanne-tarasieve.com

La Table du Joël Robuchon [136]
16, avenue Bugeaud
75016 Paris
T 56 28 16 16

La Table du Lancaster [143]
Hôtel Lancaster
7, rue de Berri
75008 Paris
T 40 76 40 18
W www.hotel-lancaster.fr

Le Temps au Temps [104]
13, rue Paul-Bert
75011 Paris
T 43 79 63 40
W http://tempsautemps.com

Théâtre de l'Atelier [72]
1, place Charles-Dullin
75018 Paris
T 46 06 19 89
E theatreatelier@theatre-
  atelier.com
W www.theatre-atelier.com

ToolsGalerie [87]
119, rue Vielle-du-Temple
75003 Paris
T 42 77 35 80
E lb@toolsgalerie.com
W www.toolsgalerie.com

Le Train Bleu [103]
Gare de Lyon
place Louis Armand
75012 Paris
T 44 75 76 76
E reservation.trainbleu@ssp.com
W www.le-train-bleu.com

Les Trois Marches de Catherine B [20]
1, rue Guisarde
75006 Paris
T 43 54 74 18
E catherine-b@catherine-b.com
W www.catherine-b.com

Le Troquet [39]
21, rue François-Bonvin
75015 Paris
T 45 66 89 00

Van Cleef & Arpels [162]
24, place Vendôme
75001 Paris
T 53 45 35 50
W www.vancleef-arpels.com

Vanessa Bruno [20]
25, rue St-Sulpice
75006 Paris
T 43 54 41 04
12, rue Castiglione
75001 Paris
T 42 61 44 60
W www.vanessabruno.com

Le Verre Volé [152]
67, rue de Lancry
75010 Paris
T 48 03 17 34

Vertical [103]
63, avenue Daumesnil
75012 Paris
T 43 40 26 26
E courrier@vertical.fr
W www.vertical.fr

VIA [103]
29–35, avenue Daumesnil
75012 Paris
T 46 28 11 11
E via@mobilier.com
W www.via.asso.fr

Viaduc des Arts [103]
1–129, avenue Daumesnil
75012 Paris

T 44 75 80 66
W www.viaduc-des-arts.com

Le Viaduc Café [103]
43, avenue Daumesnil
75012 Paris
T 44 74 70 70
E infos@viaduc-cafe.fr
W www.viaduc-cafe.fr

Le Vieux Chêne [106]
7, rue Dahomey
75011 Paris
T 43 71 67 69

Le Villaret [142]
13, rue Ternaux
75011 Paris
T 43 57 89 76

Il Vino [36]
13, boulevard de la Tour Maubourg
75007 Paris
T 44.11.72.00
E info@
  ilvinobyenricobernado.com
W www.
  ilvinobyenricobernardo.com

Ze Kitchen Galerie [144]
4, rue des Grands-Augustins
75006 Paris
T 44 32 00 32
E contact@zkg.fr
W www.zekitchengalerie.fr

Zélia sur la Terre comme au Ciel [72]
47 ter, rue d'Orsel
75018 Paris
T 46 06 96 51
E zelia@zelia.net
W www.zelia.net

ST-GERMAIN-EN-LAYE [178]
Take the RER A1, a commuter line leaving from a number of central Paris Métro stops, to St-Germain-en-Laye, about a 40-minute journey. Alternatively, take the RER A5 from a central Paris Métro stop to Poissy.

Villa Savoye
82, rue de Villiers
78300 Poissy
T 39 65 01 06
E villa-savoye@monuments-
  france.fr
W www.monuments-nationaux.fr
Open every day except Mondays

Musée Claude Debussy
38, rue au Pain
78100 St-Germain-en-Laye
T 39 73 02 64

La Forestière
1, avenue Kennedy
78100 St-Germain-en-Laye
T 30 61 64 64
E reservation@cazaudehore.fr
W www.cazaudehore.fr
Rooms from €195

BARBIZON [180]
Barbizon is most easily reached by taking a 40-minute train ride, which leaves from Gare de Lyon, to Fontainebleau. From there, it is approximately a 15-minute taxi ride to Barbizon and the hotel.

Musée Auberge du Père-Ganne
92, rue Grande
77630 Barbizon
T 60 22 27 00
E barbizon@cg77.fr

Hôtellerie du Bas-Bréau
22, rue Grande
77630 Barbizon
T 60 66 40 05
E basbreau@relaischateaux.com
W www.bas-breau.com
Rooms from €250

Vaux le Vicomte
77950 Maincy
T 64 14 41 90
E chateau@vaux-le-vicomte.com
W www.vaux-le-vicomte.com

REIMS [182]
Reims is approximately a 90-minute train journey from Paris's Gare de l'Est; trains leave about every hour. The hotel is located about ten minutes from the city centre by taxi.

Château Les Crayères
64, boulevard Henry Vasnier
51685 Reims
T 03 26 82 80 80
E reservation@lescrayeres.com
W www.gerardboyer.com
Rooms from €375

LE CHÂTEAU D'ESCLIMONT [184]
It is a 35–50-minute train journey from Gare Montparnasse to Rambouillet. From there the château is about a 20-minute taxi ride.

Le Château d'Esclimont +
Le Rochefoucauld
28700 St Symphorien le Château
T 02 37 31 15 15
E esclimont@grandesetapes.fr
W www.esclimont.com
Rooms from €150